MAGICAL
PLACES

Running Press
Hachette Book Group
1290 Avenue of the Americas, New York, NY 10104
www.runningpress.com
@Running_Press

Printed in China

First Edition: June 2019

Published by Running Press, an imprint of Perseus Books, LLC, a subsidiary
of Hachette Book Group, Inc. The Running Press name and logo is a trademark
of the Hachette Book Group.

The Hachette Speakers Bureau provides a wide range of authors for speaking
events. To find out more, go to www.hachettespeakersbureau.com or call
(866) 376-6591. The publisher is not responsible for websites (or their content)
that are not owned by the publisher.

Print book cover and interior design by Susan Van Horn

Library of Congress Control Number: 2018967237

ISBNs: 978-0-7624-6597-2 (hardcover), 978-0-7624-6598-9 (ebook)

RRD-S

10 9 8 7 6 5 4 3 2 1

MAGICAL PLACES

AN ENCHANTED JOURNEY THROUGH MYSTICAL SITES, HAUNTED HOUSES, AND FAIRYTALE FORESTS

NIKKI VAN DE CAR

ILLUSTRATIONS BY
KATIE VERNON

Running Press
PHILADELPHIA

⇥ CONTENTS ⇤

Introduction . . . 1

FAIRYTALE LOCALES . . . *3*

Hinatuan Enchanted River 4

The Fairy Glen 7

Strait of Messina 8

Knuckerhole 9

The Giant's Causeway 11

Plain of Jars 12

The City of Ys 14

Swat River 17

Pennard Castle 19

Lake Lagarfljót 20

In Search of Magic 21

Yeun Elez 23

Ha Long Bay 24

Llyn y Fan Fach 27

PLACES OF HEALING . . . *29*

Kusatsu Onsen 30

Chimayó 33

Lourdes 34

In Search of Magic 35

The Ganges River 37

Stardreaming 38

Naag Mandir 39

Killin 40

MAGIC IN NATURE . . . *43*

Hang Son Doong 45

Pink Lakes 46

Cave of the Crystals 47

Sea of Stars 48

In Search of Magic 48

Tianzi Mountain 51

Mont Saint-Michel 52

Salar de Uyuni 53

Gorëme. 54

To Sua Trench. 56

Crooked Forest 57

Waitomo 59

The Door to Hell 60

HAUNTED PLACES . . . 63

Pantéon de Belén 64

Ballyboley Forest. 65

The Paris Catacombs 67

Salem. 68

In Search of Magic 69

Davelis Cave. 70

Island of the Dolls 72

Devil's Gate Dam. 73

Cannock Chase 74

Poveglia. 76

Bell Witch Cave 77

Bhangarh Ruins 79

Dudley Castle. 80

Ma-no Umi 81

The Pine Barrens 82

New Orleans 84

THE PAST IN THE PRESENT . . . 87

Reykjavik 88

Hafnarfjöròur. 89

Graz. 90

Taipei 92

Saidai-ji Temple 93

Madagascar 95

Mari El Republic. 96

Mexico City 98

In Search of Magic 100

Ni'ihau 101

KwaZulu-Natal 102

EARTH CHAKRAS ... 105

Mount Shasta 107

In Search of Magic 109

Lake Titicaca 113

Uluru 114

Stonehenge 117

The Great Pyramid 120

Glastonbury Tor 122

Mount Kailash 125

LEY LINES ... 127

Wistman's Wood 129

Kukaniloko 130

Haleakalā 131

Bali 132

Palenque 135

Sedona 136

Angkor Wat 138

Mount Fuji 141

In Search of Magic 142

Lake Taupo 143

Table Mountain 144

Conclusion ... 146

Acknowledgments ... 147

Photo Credits ... 148

Index ... 149

⇥ INTRODUCTION ⇤

There are times when the world seems, shall we say, prosaic. The gas station, the strip mall, the suburb—it feels like none of these places could ever be remotely magical and, worse, that their very existence, and our existence within them, makes it impossible for magic to exist at all.

But there are places in the world where magic has been, and still is, an everyday reality, a part of life. There are sacred springs renowned for their healing properties; forests teeming with the supernatural; homes of fairies, dragons, and other mythical creatures; sites where ancient magical rites are still practiced; and centers of profound energetic and mystical power.

Unsurprisingly, these places are frequently astonishingly beautiful.

From Stonehenge to the Hang Son Doong in Vietnam, from the Door to Hell in Turkmenistan to the Giant's Causeway in Ireland, there is evidence of magic everywhere. And while these incredible locations aren't always easy to get to (like the Cave of the Crystals in Naica, Mexico), as armchair voyagers we will be able to make our own pilgrimage, bringing the magic of these places into our lives, wherever we are.

FAIRYTALE LOCALES

THERE ARE PLACES IN THE WORLD WHERE DRAGONS HAVE slithered and giants have battled. There are places where fairies dwell and spirits keep watch.

Or so legend has it. People have always told stories to explain what seemed unexplainable at the time. We find oddly perfect basalt columns formed by ancient lava flows and decide that giants must have built them. A river so impossibly clear we can barely fathom it must hold naiads and other water spirits. Countless mountains around the world are ancient beings turned to stone or homes of the gods.

Not too many generations ago, these kinds of natural phenomena were often viewed as acts of vengeful or, less often, generous gods. Now we say that they are geothermal, volcanic, weather-based, or built by ancient civilizations. Who is to say that our new, scientific explanations won't be called into question a few more generations down the line? Our reasoning—our storytelling—may one day be considered equally fanciful.

For now, let's let go of reason, unleash our imaginations, and walk among the fairies.

HINATUAN ENCHANTED RIVER

THE HINATUAN RIVER, ON THE ISLAND OF MINDANAO IN THE Philippines, is very short. For a brief 2,000 feet, its waters stretch toward the Pacific Ocean—and within that tiny distance runs the clearest river water in the world. It is as smooth as glass, and you can see the bottom at even its deepest points—which can be as great as eighty feet. Swimming in its crystalline waters feels like flying.

The river stays so clear because it is fed by underground caverns; the majority of the Hinatuan is subterranean, which keeps the water filtered and pure until it emerges right at its end. There, it blends with the nearby ocean, forming a brackish mix. That underground cave system has only added to the river's mystery, of course.

The mystical Hinatuan has inspired a lot of folklore. Locals believe that it is the various spirits who watch over the river that keep its waters so clear. *Engkanto* (mermaids) have often been seen frolicking in its waters, and the fish that swim in it cannot be caught, by any means, it is said—and if such a miracle would occur, the fisherman would be cursed. Even the acacia and balete trees on the river's banks are enchanted, as they are home to *diwata*, Filipino tree spirits. All of the various creatures that dwell in and around the Enchanted River are reputedly unearthly, beautiful, and benevolent—but less so at night. Night is *their* time with the river, and several unexplained drownings have been blamed on *engkanto* or *diwata*.

Specific parts of the river are also said to be forbidden territory, day or night: In certain places, where the river spirits are particularly unwelcoming, swimmers can develop rashes or scratches, and some have reported feeling pulled beneath the water by an unseen force. Others have been lured into the surrounding woods. Locals say this happens when proper respect is not given to nature.

For this reason, those places are forbidden, and access to the entire river, otherwise serene and welcoming, is cut off after dark.

THE FAIRY GLEN

THE FAIRY GLEN ON THE ISLE OF SKYE IN Scotland is but a tiny valley between two small villages. And while there are no specific legends surrounding the glen, the landscape itself is otherworldly. (Not that there isn't plenty of fairy folklore to go around on Skye; nearby Castle Dunvegan displays an ancient, tattered flag symbolizing the clan's truce with the fairies, from a time when human-fairy relations were as real and practical as keeping an eye on the weather.)

The Fairy Glen is dipped with tiny lochs and dotted with hills, the tallest of which still has its basalt column from the island's formation. From a distance, it looks like the ruin of some ancient tower, and so it is nicknamed "Castle Ewan." Behind the "castle," nestled in its low cliff, is a tiny cave. Visitors press pennies into its crevices for good luck.

There are more waterfalls, strange rock formations, unusual steppes, and odd little hills than really ought to exist in such a small area, but according to geologists this is all because of a very natural landslide long ago. The large rings of stones found in the glen are likely not *actual* fairy rings, those magical portals through which unsuspecting humans disappear into fairyland—though many visitors experience a shiver when stepping into them! It is more likely that these rings were built by humans; the larger ones date back to early times, but the smaller ones are often built by visiting tourists. The locals tend to dismantle them once tourist season is over—they do this out of respect for the natural beauty of the place—and perhaps for its fairy inhabitants as well.

STRAIT OF MESSINA

MOST OF US ARE NOT ALL THAT UP ON OUR HOMER, BUT WE know the basic gist: Circe—the witch who turned all of Odysseus's men to pigs—his time with Calypso and Nausicaä . . . generally speaking, his adventures seem to have been a bit more philandering than adventurous. But there was that time he had to choose between two far more dangerous women: Scylla and Charybdis. Scylla was a man-eating monster dwelling on one shore, and Charybdis was a whirlpool swirling close to the opposite shore. Odysseus chose Scylla, and lost six of his men.

Here's the thing: this tale isn't entirely fictional. The idea that there really was a giant woman on the shores of Messina who liked an occasional sailor-snack is perhaps unlikely, but the whirlpool Charybdis was real and is still there today. The Strait of Messina, the narrow strip of sea between Sicily and the southern tip of Italy, appears to be peaceful, but in reality it is frequently an absolute mess. It sits between the Tyrrhenian and Ionian Seas, and their opposing currents do often stir up whirlpools, known locally as *garofali*. They aren't by any means big enough to sink a ship and any boat with a motor would have little trouble navigating them, but they're a bit intimidating nonetheless!

KNUCKERHOLE

THERE ARE A NUMBER OF KNUCKERHOLES TO BE FOUND IN various places, but the most famous is in Lyminster, England. This knuckerhole, a pond which neither freezes in winter nor dries up in the summer, is apparently bottomless—six bell ropes from a nearby church were once dropped down into the depths to measure it, but the bottom was never reached.

What is a knuckerhole, exactly? A knuckerhole is occupied by—you guessed it—a knucker: an enormous, legless water dragon. It kills like a python by squeezing its prey to death or by shredding flesh with its enormous fangs—or it did. Tales about knuckers date back to Saxon oral traditions, and in fact the name *knucker* is derived from the Old English *nicor*—which referred to any kind of water-dwelling monster. One popular story tells of a knucker in Lyminster, who was slain by a local village boy. The boy came up with an odd yet effective plan: with the assistance of the village mayor, young Jim baked an enormous pie and filled it with poison. Using a cart and horse, Jim hauled the giant pie out to the knuckerhole and then ran away to a hiding place. It's a good thing he did, too, since the knucker ate not only the pie, but the cart and horse as well. Still, the poison did the trick, killing the knucker, and Jim chopped off its head just in case.

There is a gravestone in St. Mary Magdalene Church in Lyminster called The Slayer's Slab, dedicated to the hero who killed the knucker, and the waters of the knuckerhole are still occasionally consumed as a healing tonic.

THE GIANT'S CAUSEWAY

THERE ARE AROUND 40,000 INTERLOCKING ROCK columns on the Antrim Coast of Northern Ireland. The official, geological explanation is that these basalt formations are remnants of an ancient volcano. Most of the columns are hexagonal, but there are octagons and septagons as well. Over millions of years of weathering, some of the stones have come to resemble objects and have received loving nicknames, like the Organ, Giant's Boot, the Honeycomb, and the Giant's Gate.

The legend is that these stones—so like steps in their shape and organization—were in fact a bridge built by the Irish giant Fionn mac Cumhaill. The story goes that another giant, the Scottish Benandonner, challenged Fionn to a duel (historically, Scots and Irish never really got along, and apparently giants were no exception) and this causeway was built so that the two could cross the channel and meet in battle.

Depending on who is telling the story, Fionn either defeats Benandonner or runs and hides when he sees how much larger the Scottish giant is than he. In the latter version, Fionn's wife Oonagh disguises him as a baby in a cradle and warns Benandonner that if this is the son, how much larger must the father be? And so Benandonner flees Ireland, destroying the causeway in his wake so that Fionn can't follow him. In either version, Fionn mac Cumhaill comes out the winner, using either brains or brawn—as suits Irish heroes.

Across the sea, at Fingal's Cave in Scotland, you can find identical basalt deposits—or the other end of the ruined causeway.

PLAIN OF JARS

THROUGHOUT THE COUNTRYSIDE OF LAOS
you'll find scattered thousands of giant prehistoric jars. They vary in height from three to nine
feet, are made mostly from sandstone, and date
back to the Iron Age. They have a kind of a lip, as
if they were meant to have lids, but the majority
of those lids seem to have been made from animal skins and so have been lost to time.

Local legend tells of a race of giants ruled
by Khun Cheung, who in celebration of his many
victories brewed Lao-Lao, a kind of rice wine,
in the jars. Presumably, he and his compatriots
drank *a lot.*

But the prevailing, scientific theory is that
the jars were used in a kind of burial ritual, as
bones and beads have been found nearby—but
never inside the vessels. Perhaps they were a
kind of fermentation container for preserving
bodies? Or perhaps they were crematoriums?

The answers to these questions are almost
impossible to find out, as Laos is filled with unex-
ploded ordnance left over from the Vietnam
War, making excavation extremely dangerous.
There are ninety known sites, but only a few of
them are safe to access, limiting research.

THE CITY OF YS

A BEAUTIFUL AND VIBRANT FRENCH CITY ON THE BAY OF Douarnenez in Brittany, Ys thrived from its first moments. But over thousands of years, erosion from the sea made it vulnerable to flooding. Around the fourth century AD, King Gradlon, a recently converted Christian, controlled the tidal surges by building a dike around the city with gates that could open and close, allowing ships to enter and depart. The gates were locked with a key, held by the king himself.

Ys was a wealthy city, and King Gradlon's castle was made of cedar, marble, and gold. The city was widely respected for its art and beauty, but that regard began to dwindle as Christianity took hold throughout Europe. Although King Gradlon had converted thanks to the efforts of St. Winwaloe, his people had not—and neither had his daughter Dahut. She remained a devout Druid and continued to worship the old gods, particularly that of the sea. As pressure from the Church increased, rumors began to spread about Dahut. These were, unsurprisingly, fairly salacious in nature. They claimed that she took lovers, made them wear a black satin mask that strangled them in the night (once she was done with them, of course), and then gave their bodies to the sea as tribute. St. Winwaloe urged Gradlon to rein in his daughter, but despite his newfound faith, he refused. He loved her.

One day, a Red Knight rode into the city. Dahut was instantly infatuated with him and, after a night of merrymaking, took him to her bed. Her love for him was such that she didn't make him wear the deadly satin mask (if she ever asked such a thing of any lover), and the seas at the city walls were wild with their passion. Wanting to see the storm, the Red Knight insisted they open the gates, and Dahut stole the key from her sleeping father.

The waves surged through the gap, flooding the city. King Gradlon awoke to find his key gone and understood instantly what must have happened. He jumped on a magic horse named Morvac'h that was able to gallop through the sea and lifted Dahut up behind him, intent on bringing her to safety despite her betrayal. But with Dahut astride, Morvac'h could not break free of the waves. St. Winwaloe told Gradlon that Dahut was a demon and must be cast off, or she would drown them all. Gradlon regretfully did so, and he, St. Winwaloe, and Morvac'h rode to safety.

Gradlon set up residence in the nearby town of Quimper, and a statue of Gradlon and Morvac'h still stands in its cathedral today. Dahut, it is said, did not drown, but was transformed into a morgen, a Breton water spirit in the tradition of sirens and mermaids, while the entire of city of Ys was swept under the sea, where Dahut now rules as its queen. When the waters are calm, the people of Breton claim you can hear the bells of Ys tolling beneath the water. Legend says that when Paris (which translates to "like Ys" in Breton) sinks, Ys will rise again.

SWAT RIVER

THE SWAT RIVER IN PAKISTAN IS HOME
to Apalala, a powerful naga or water dragon, who
controls the rainfall and its resulting rivers. Unlike
most dragons, he has a human head, along with a
serpentine body—as such, Apalala is both wise and
cunning and has an affinity for humans. He pro-
tects his people from other, less benevolent dragons and ensures a good harvest with just the right
amount of rain.

The Swat Province of Pakistan is rich with early
Buddhist lore, and there are several variations of
Apalala's story. One legend says that he did his
work so well that the people forgot about him—or
at least took him for granted. They stopped giving him his yearly tribute . . . and while Apalala is
kind, like most of us he doesn't take well to being
ignored. In anger, he flooded the villages, and
this went on for some time. So the Buddha came
to Pakistan with Vajrapani, Buddha's guide and a
symbol of his power. Vajrapani smote the steep
mountains above the Swat River, intimidating the
powerful naga. Buddha reminded Apalala of his
compassion, and Apalala converted to Buddhism.
Since that time he asks for tribute only once every
twelve years. And so, every twelve years, the
rain falls heavy, and the flooded crop that rises is
Apalala's tribute.

PENNARD CASTLE

PENNARD CASTLE IN WALES WAS BUILT AROUND THE TWELFTH century, but it was abandoned only 200 years later. While Pennard, being quite small and primitive, was likely never the most comfortable of castles, in those days people didn't just leave perfectly good shelters without reason. And there is nothing in the surrounding geography to explain its desertion. Some have argued that the nearby sand dunes might have made it an uncomfortable place in the wind, but that doesn't seem to be quite enough to justify leaving a sound and strategically useful castle standing empty.

There are other theories, of course. Local lore tells us that sometime in the fourteenth century, the castle was held by a baron who had just won a significant battle for his king—as his reward, he was to be given the king's daughter's hand in marriage. The daughter in question was said to "spend time with fairies." This could have been an unfortunate euphemism for being slow-witted or a literal description of her activities. Either way it might have been of concern to the baron, but she was still a princess after all.

The wedding was suitably raucous and drunken for a post-battle affair. In fact, the baron and his men were so severely intoxicated that when mysterious, sparkling lights were spotted outside the castle walls, they all rushed out, swords in hand, to mow down the intruders.

The lights, of course, belonged to the fairies, who had come to attend the princess. They were not harmed by the attack—but they were severely offended. As the baron and his men realized what they had done, a sharp wind began to blow. It whipped up the surrounding sand, lashing and killing them, and stripping the castle to ruins overnight.

What became of the princess is unknown.

LAKE LAGARFLJÓT

LAKE LAGARFLJÓT IN ICELAND IS HOME TO NOT ONE, BUT *two* water-dwelling monsters. The first and largest is relatively unknown. He is called Skirimsl and was a giant serpent who wreaked havoc upon the people of Iceland until, in a story similar to St. George and his dragon, Gudmund the Good chained him to the floor of the deep lake. Skirimsl will not break free until Doomsday . . . at which point we'll have a lot of other problems.

The smaller dragon is a kind of lindworm (translated: heath snake); a creature with a serpentine body and two clawed arms at the front, so that it kind of slither-crawls along when on land. The Lagarfljót lindworm did start life on land; it was captured by a girl when she was very young. She had been given a golden ring, and following the advice of her mother, she caught the lindworm and locked it in her linen chest with the ring—perhaps the idea was that the magic of the lindworm would transfer over to the ring.

But something went awry with her plan, and the lindworm grew astonishingly quickly. Within a matter of days, it broke out of its prison, and the girl was forced to hurl the chest, complete with lindworm and ring, into Lake Lagarfljót. There, the creature continued to grow and to torment anyone who entered its waters.

The Lagarfljót lindworm is still sometimes spotted to this day, and the sightings foretell a year of terrible weather and equally terrible harvests.

IN SEARCH OF MAGIC

A *lot* of stories about the magical places of this world involve dragons— way more than are featured here in this book. Dragons, by one name or another, feature in just about every culture on Earth, from the *moʻolele* of Hawaiʻi, naga of Pakistan, and *sárkány* of Hungary to *lóng* in China, *ryū* in Japan, and many, many more.

The obvious theory, of course, is that our ancestors found the bones of dinosaurs. But the stories are often eerily similar, with tales of protection, battle, magical blood, death, and destruction. Why have so many cultures gravitated toward these same kinds of tales? In much the same way, just about every culture on Earth has a Rumpelstiltskin/Loki/Coyote/Anansi figure, a Baba Yaga figure, and a Beauty and the Beast story, among many other overlapping archetypes. What is the dragon figure in your indigenous culture? What magic can you glean from it?

You'll find that most watering holes or rivers in an area will have a legend around them. Seek them out! Poke around on the Internet, or even better, stop by a retirement home or that coffee shop where folks who have lived in the same town for generations hang out. You might find that the most prosaic, familiar places suddenly feel so much more mysterious and magical than before.

YEUN ELEZ

NOT FAR FROM NORMANDY'S MONT Saint-Michel, flooded by the same tides that create that island's quicksand, is the marshland of Yeun Elez. It is known as the Gates of Hell, and it is here that Ankou, the Breton personification of death, would come to fetch lost souls in his cart, bringing them to Youdig, the bottomless bog at the heart of the marsh. The marsh is said to be filled with Ankou's associates, including goblins, elves, and korrigans, all of which hope to lure unsuspecting travelers to Ankou's clutches.

There are contemporary accounts of priests performing exorcisms in the area and then leading the cast-out devils to the marsh so that they could return from whence they came. On the night of the Sabbath, members of the clergy would cast the demons into the bodies of black dogs and then release them into the bog. The priests would then lie facedown in the muck until sunrise, so that they would not be witness to anything that occurred. If they looked up, they would be dragged into Youdig as well.

The marsh occasionally still winks with will-o'-the-wisps, small or sometimes large peat fires caused by lightning strikes. Visitors to Yeun Elez do occasionally get lost in its heavy mists, and local Druids perform ceremonies at its edge to ensure peace and safety for those who live nearby.

HA LONG BAY

HA LONG BAY IN VIETNAM IS SURROUNDED BY TWO THOUSAND sharp, steep little islets. These tiny limestone islands are often hollow, sheltering grottoes or even lakes within them, and many have spawned individual legends. But the story of the bay itself dates back to early Vietnamese culture and its connections with *rongs*—enormous, snakelike flying dragons that are believed to hold jewels in their mouths.

Attacked by invaders from the North, the Vietnamese people fled the villages surrounding Ha Long Bay, believing all was hopeless. But their gods watched from above, and sent a mother *rong* and her children to defend the people. The dragons descended from the sky, striking terror into the hearts of the invaders. They spat their jewels into the seas surrounding Vietnam, and the jewels sprang up into islands, forming a wall of protection that defends Vietnam to this day. *Ha Long* translates to "Descending Dragon." Following their great rescue, the *rongs* stayed on Earth rather than returning to heaven, maintaining the peace and bringing good luck.

Thien Cung Grotto, one of the largest of the hollow islets, was home to the king of the *rongs*. During a drought, a young couple came to beseech the king, and he graciously brought the rain. This couple's daughter, May, fell in love with the king's son, the Dragon Prince. Their wedding held in the center of the grotto was celebrated for seven days and seven nights and attended by animals and people of all kinds. Elephants, snakes, dragons, genies, birds, and fish danced and sang, and their figures can still be seen, fossilized in the stalactites and stalagmites of the cave. At the back of the cave are three clear ponds of water fed by a gushing stream. Here is where May bathed her 100 children; once they reached adolescence, she led fifty of them out into the wild to seek new lands. The other fifty remained, and legend holds that modern-day Vietnamese are their descendants.

LLYN Y FAN FACH

WALES IS COVERED IN LAKES, BUT THIS ONE IS special. Llyn y Fan Fach is said to be the origin of the Lady of the Lake—the woman who gave King Arthur the sword Excalibur.

She had her own backstory, though, which dates to the eleventh or twelfth century and is recorded in one of history's oldest books, the *Red Book of Hergest*. Before she tried her hand at king making, the lady in question was sitting on a rock near the lake, when a local farmer fell in love with her. He tried three times to woo her, and after the third she finally relented, but with a caveat: if he hit her three times, she would return to the lake.

Now, regrettably, hitting one's wife was a regular pastime at this point in history. Still the farmer loved her so much that he agreed to her condition. But, surprise, surprise: he couldn't stick to it. Being that the lady was magical, she didn't behave as normal people did, and the farmer responded the only way he knew how. When she cried at the christening of their firstborn (because she knew her baby would be harmed by the sun), he hit her. When she cried at the wedding of a neighbor (because she knew he would die soon), he hit her. And when she laughed at that neighbor's funeral (because she knew his suffering had come to an end), he hit her once more.

She immediately fled back to the lake, and the farmer, full of regret, could do nothing to stop her. But her three sons, including the one with sensitivity to the sun, inherited her powers. They started a dynasty of herbalists known as the Physicians of Myddfai, who still practice today.

PLACES OF HEALING

THE WORLD IS FILLED WITH HEALING SPRINGS, GROVES, *forests, and patches of earth. For so many cultures, and so many different beliefs, they inform a way of life. Those listed here are by no means all of them—nor are they even all the most famous. But this collection of sites is a fairly inclusive representation of the types of locations famous for their therapeutic properties.*

Most places of healing involve water. Perhaps this is because water sustains all life—so it would certainly follow that it would cure all life. Natural hot springs like those at Kusatsu Onsen, Japan, can increase blood flow and metabolism, give the body essential minerals, and theoretically eradicate some diseases. Other waters are famous for more religious reasons, like the spring at Lourdes or the Ganges River.

Indeed, second to water, it is religions and beliefs of various types that provide context for places of healing, including Chimayó, New Mexico, and Killin, Scotland. And then there are some locales that are just kind of odd, like Naag Mandir in Fiji and Stardreaming in New Mexico.

Do any of these places have an empirically measurable effect? Science says not particularly. But people have been healed—or believe they have been healed—by them for centuries, and all of these sites are still visited, and still provide relief, to this day.

KUSATSU ONSEN

SINCE THE EDO PERIOD BETWEEN 1603 AND 1868, THE RITUALS of bathing in *onsen*, or hot springs, have been considered to be somewhere between a healing and spiritual experience in Japan. Depending on the mineral content of the spring in question, it is believed that it can provide relief for just about anything—many claim that lovesickness is the only thing a soak in *onsen* cannot cure. In the town of Kusatsu, the *onsen* is highly acidic—so much so, in fact, that an aluminum yen coin would dissolve completely after soaking there for a week. The mineral content, or *yo no hana*, in Kusatsu Onsen is said to heal wounds, muscle sprains, poor circulation, and much more, and so the baths were visited often by samurai and shogun.

There are three separate rituals, all intended to ready the bather for the acidity and the extremely hot temperatures—in their natural state, the *onsen* sit at about 150 degrees Fahrenheit. The bather washes first, prays, and enters the bath unclothed.

> JIKAN-YU ◆ First, attendants perform *yumomi*; using long, flat paddles, they stir the water to aerate it, cooling it to a comparatively tepid 118 degrees. This also stimulates the minerals in the water, so that they will settle around the bather's body, offering some protection from the heat. The bather places a towel over their head and kneels as hot water is repeatedly poured over the skull to activate the cerebellum as the part of the brain that controls the body's temperature. This dilates the blood vessels, preventing blood from rushing to the head when the bather enters the pool. When ready, the bather then goes into the water for exactly three minutes or until their face becomes bright red.

> AGARI-YU ◆ After soaking in the acidic waters, the bather rinses in an alkaline bath to regain balance and improve skin tone.

> AWASE-YU ◆ This method is particularly good for circulation. The bather starts in a relatively cool 100-degree pool, moving gradually through five separate baths, until reaching 115 degrees, and then starts over.

After bathing, visitors drink warm fluids such as tea and sit wrapped in a steamed towel to retain the heat of the *onsen* for as long as possible and to allow sweat and impurities to drain out of the body.

CHIMAYÓ

THE CATHOLIC CHURCH IN CHIMAYÓ, NEW MEXICO, IS QUITE small, but it attracts over 300,000 visitors a year, making it the most important Catholic pilgrimage site in the United States.

El Santuario de Chimayó was built around a hole in the ground. In the early 1800s, a priest named Don Bernardo Abeyta saw a burning light on a hillside. When he went to investigate the source of the light, he found a crucifix buried in the dirt. He brought the crucifix down to the village, but it disappeared—only to be found again in the same hole. This happened twice more, until finally the villagers got the message and built their church around the site.

Once the church was erected, the miraculous healings began. That first church was almost immediately replaced by a larger adobe shrine in 1816—and this is the site visitors go to today. The hole remains, and the dirt continues to be blessed and to heal those who require it. This well of dirt is known as *el pocito*, and it is in a low anteroom off the side of the altar. Visitors must stoop to get in. There, they may kneel and reach into the unassuming, unadorned hole in the ground to scoop up dirt. It can be rubbed on an afflicted area, boiled into tea, thrown into a fire to avert a natural disaster, and more. The *tierra bendita*, or blessed dirt, is believed to have cured cancer, overcome infertility, and reversed blindness and the course of multiple sclerosis.

As visitors exit the room holding *el pocito*, they pass a wall of abandoned, no-longer-required crutches, small shrines, crosses, and scrap after scrap of paper testifying to the power of El Santuario de Chimayó.

LOURDES

IT IS IMPOSSIBLE TO MENTION CATHOLIC HEALING SITES WITHOUT including Lourdes. In 1858, Bernadette Soubirous, a fourteen-year-old miller's daughter, had a vision. A young woman, dressed in white with a rosary and yellow roses on each foot, appeared in the grotto of Massabielle near the miller's home. Bernadette was with her sister and a neighbor, but neither of the other girls saw a thing. Bernadette and her sister were beaten for telling tales of the woman in white and forbidden from visiting the grotto. But Bernadette returned anyway, again and again. On one of her visits, the lady ordered her to dig in the ground and drink from the spring she found there. So Bernadette dug, and indeed there was a small, clear-running spring.

The miracles began, and Bernadette's visits to the grotto became pilgrimages—she was rarely alone, sometimes accompanied by as many as 9,000 people.

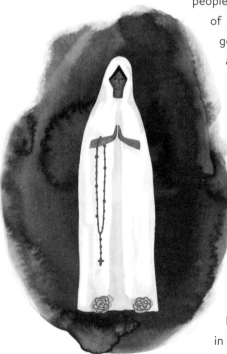

But the Church was not convinced of her power, and neither was the French government. The grotto was fenced off, and entry was forbidden. Nevertheless, Bernadette persisted, and saw the lady one last time—her eighteenth vision. When Napoleon ordered the grotto reopened and visitors returned, Bernadette was not one of them. She never went back to the grotto and never saw the lady again, but worked at a hospice until her death at age thirty-five. She was canonized by the Catholic Church in 1933.

Catherine Latapie was the first to experience a miracle at Lourdes. Her hand had seized after an injury, but a dip in the spring returned her to full mobility.

Shortly thereafter, Louis Bouriette regained vision in his right eye. There are dozens more stories of sudden healing at Lourdes, but these last two are the most dramatic: Gabriel Gargam, who had been paralyzed in a train accident in 1899, rose and walked again after bathing in the waters of Lourdes, and John Traynor, whose brain, arms, and legs were riddled with shrapnel after fighting in World War I, bathed nine times at Lourdes and returned to near-complete health.

The Church never went so far as to formally encourage visitors to view the water at Lourdes as holy, but it is nevertheless regarded as nonliturgical holy water. Since Bernadette's visions, thousands of people have made the pilgrimage to the spring to drink from it and bathe in it. Chemical analysis of the spring has determined it to be quite pure and inert, containing no unusual minerals or substances—but at times the water has grown to be quite murky and germ-ridden, as it was bathed in again and again by the sick and the injured. These days the water is filtered and purified, and while it does flow from the source Bernadette uncovered, it is available to visitors through a series of taps.

IN SEARCH OF MAGIC

One should never appropriate the rituals of another culture or religion, but the nondenominational, personal use of water for healing is not only perfectly acceptable, but also a harmless, and occasionally powerful, ritual.

You can create that ritual in any way you like. You can fill a bowl of purified water and leave it to charge in the moonlight before bathing your face in it. You can seek out what's known as "wild water," either from a nearby stream or even the dew that collects on the grass outside, and spread some on your eyelids, or on a bruise, your temples, or anywhere that you feel might benefit from some extra healing energy.

THE GANGES RIVER

THE GANGES FLOWS THROUGH INDIA AND BANGLADESH, AND serves as a lifeline for the millions of people who dwell on her shores. The Ganges is known as the goddess Ganga in the Hindu pantheon, and all along her course, Hindus bathe in the waters as they pay homage to their gods and ancestors, cupping the water and letting it fall back into the river as a whole. They make offerings of flowers and rose petals and light shallow clay dishes of oil to float along with the current. If worshippers do not live nearby, they make pilgrimages, and bring back Ganga jal, jugs filled with water, to use in rituals at home. And, for those who are simply too far away or are unable to travel, any river can be transmuted into Ganga simply by invoking her, because the Ganges is the embodiment of all sacred waters.

Today, the Ganges is crowded and polluted. She flows crystal clear from her source in the Himalayas, but as the river winds through the industrial city of Kanpur, the waters turn dark gray, and then red, as sewage and tannery runoff drain unfiltered into the river.

But, despite that, the river's power remains. In late May or early June of each year comes Ganga Dashahara, the celebration of the descent of Ganga from the heavens to the Earth. Millions of people throng to the Ganges, for on this day a bather may wash away ten sins, or even ten lifetimes of sins. The Ganges washes away all impurities, removing them, cleansing the bather, and taking the sins away with it.

Since Ganga came from heaven, she acts as a gateway for the dead to return there. The Ganges allows Hindu people to redeem the bodies of their loved ones, either by immersing their ashes in the Ganges or in another body of water representing it.

STARDREAMING

STARDREAMING IS A COLLECTION OF OVER TWENTY (AND COUNTING)
open-air temples and labyrinths, spanning twenty-two acres on James Jereb's
property outside Santa Fe, New Mexico. Jereb is a visual artist and writer and
was called upon by ascended spiritual masters from a variety of religions to build
these temples or, as he sometimes calls them, stargates. In order to construct
them, 600 tons of stone, in 50 different varieties, were brought in from various
parts of the United States and Mexico, ranging in size from huge boulders of
granite and quartz to small chips of jasper and obsidian.

Each of the temples is different and oriented to a different stellar, lunar, or
solar alignment, according to the Hermetic tradition of geometry, including the
Fibonacci sequence. The temples include:

- Temple of the Moon
- Temple of Avalon
- Rainbow Whale Altar
- Temple of Dreams
- Temple of the Sun

- Temple of the Rainbow
  Serpent
- Temple of the Milky Way
- Temple of the Violet
  Flame
- Faery Ring
- Temple of the Heart
- Temple of Lightning

- Temple of Infinity
- Temple of the Stars
- Temple of Illumination
- Sanctuary of Ancestors
- Talking Stones
- Temple of New Atlantis
- Medicine Wheel
- Temple of Magic
- Thirteen Grandmothers

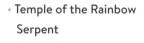

Each temple has its own function and
healing methodology—though every visi-
tor experiences it differently. The Center
of Illumination, an inner sanctum at Stardreaming, is a room filled with Jereb's
paintings and "light, sound, and frequency."

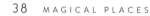

NAAG MANDIR

NAAG MANDIR IS A TEMPLE SURROUNDING A ROCK IN FIJI—A HIGHLY
unusual rock. The rock is shaped like a rearing, hooded cobra, and it is growing.

In the early 1900s, an elderly man named Alju visited a rock in the jungle, one that was rumored to be getting larger. Alju and a few other villagers worshipped the stone, laying flowers, milk, and fruit at its base, as it grew beneath a guava tree. At the time, it was only about three feet high. They believed the rock to be a representation of Naag Baba, a Hindu snake god.

In the 1930s, a nonnative government official working on a new road in the area ordered the stone bulldozed. The bulldozer operator, a Fijian and Hindu, refused, so the official tried to bulldoze the rock himself. He could not do it—no matter what he tried, the rock remained untouched, and legend has it the official died that night.

This, of course, lent credence to stories of the stone's power, and it continued to be worshipped as it continued to grow. By 1969, it had pushed past its guava tree cover, and locals built a tin shack to protect it from the elements. But by then, the rock was growing at an alarming rate, and in 1972, another structure had to be erected to protect the now eight-foot-tall stone. This structure, unfortunately, was made of concrete, and the stone quickly outgrew it, so that by 1975 an extension had to be constructed to accommodate the twelve-foot-high stone.

After this, worshippers pleaded with the stone to slow down, and since 1975 the stone's rate of growth is only about half an inch per year. This slower rate has allowed worshippers to build a dedicated, permanent temple in a gorgeous riot of color with the stone itself draped in flower garlands and surrounded by offerings.

The rock is believed to cure the sick and infertile, as snakes represent death and rebirth.

KILLIN

AROUND AD 700, FILLAN (MEANING "LITTLE WOLF") WAS BORN TO
the house of Ulster, a pre-Christian kingdom in Northern Ireland. Legend has it
that he was born with a stone in his mouth, which so disturbed his father, Prince
Federach, that he was tossed into the river. The baby was rescued by Bishop Ibar,
who watched over him and raised him in a monastery.

St. Fillan's miracles began early. The monastery, being characteristically aus-
tere, forbade the use of candles after dark—but St. Fillan liked to read into the
night. His left arm and hand glowed upon command, a power he retained until
his death. St. Fillan traveled to Scotland, living in and around Killin, spreading the
word of God. (His glowing arm and hand, kept as relics, were considered so powerful that they are credited with Robert the Bruce's success at freeing Scotland
from British rule.)

He built a priory and a mill there, which he managed himself. One day, as
St. Fillan was plowing, his ox was attacked and killed by a wolf . . . who then
lamented his error and offered to be yoked in the oxen's place. St. Fillan and

the wolf worked at the mill and priory until the
end of their days, creating a number of healing resources, some of which are still in use
today. (To request a healing from St. Fillan, walk three times around his well, and
drop a stone into its depths.) There's also
St. Fillan's Holy Pool nearby, but it is less
popular nowadays. At one time, it was
used to heal the insane. They were dunked
into the pool and then strapped onto a pew
in the priory overnight.

Upon his death, St. Fillan left eight
healing stones, along with some other relics
(including his arm bone, of course). The largest and roundest is the head stone, which can

cure any problems relating to the head, including loss of vision, headache, and mental illness. Two nearly identical, flat stones are used to treat problems with the front of the torso or the back (you can tell which is which because one has a small indentation in the center, like a navel). The five remaining stones are intended for healing the arms and legs.

The stones are now kept in the walls of St. Fillan's mill, resting on a bed of leaves, twigs, and river detritus, which is replaced every year at Christmas Eve.

MAGIC IN NATURE

TECHNICALLY, NONE OF THESE LOCATIONS ARE ACTUALLY MAGICAL; *all can be explained by geology, biology, or chemistry. But they are so unlikely, so strange, unusual, and frequently astonishingly beautiful, that they feel magical.*

From holes in the ground deep enough to dive into to crystals as large as a city bus, from sand that can swallow a galloping horse to the eternal flame in Turkmenistan—all of these wonders can be seen and explained, but they still don't quite seem real. There is a kind of magic in the natural world, a magic that has only recently been explained by science—which is, in itself, just another form of magic.

HANG SON DOONG

IMAGINE A CAVE SO MASSIVE A 747 COULD fly into it. Hang Son Doong in Vietnam, the largest cave on Earth, is so big it has its own weather system. Clouds form within its depths, fed by a fast-flowing subterranean river. The cave has its own small jungle, which formed after the roof of a cavern collapsed, allowing enough light for life to prosper. Hornbills, flying foxes, monkeys, and other creatures make their home there, underground.

Hang Son Doong was discovered in 1991 by a local man named Khanh looking for wood in the jungle, but as its descent is extremely steep, he left and wasn't able to find it again until 2009. Fewer people have entered this cavern than have stood on Mount Everest.

Stalactites and stalagmites as long as 230 feet adorn the floor and ceiling, so tall you could climb up them, and droplets of water from the jungle above have formed cave pearls the size of baseballs. Hang Son Doong is between two and five million years old, and parts of it have never flooded in all that time, leaving fossils in near-perfect condition.

LAKE RETBA OF SENEGAL AND LAKE HILLIER OF AUSTRALIA are called the pink lakes—and they are not just slightly tinged. They are a Valentine's Day candy hearts kind of pink. They are not the only pink lakes in the world, but they are the largest and most pigmented. Pink lakes take on this unusual color because of their high salinity; they are formed just off the ocean's coast. They tend to contain as much salt as the Dead Sea, so much that locals harvest the salt by simply scooping it up from the bottom. That salt content attracts bacteria known as *Dunaliella salina* as well as halobacteria, and together, these organisms produce the pink hue. Humans can swim in these lakes without harm, but no creatures can survive in their waters; the bacteria are the only organism able to live in such high quantities of salt, so there are no competitors.

There is a bit of a mystery around Lake Hillier. Lake Retba and the other pink lakes of the world tend to get diluted during the rainy season, losing their pinkish hue, but Lake Hillier does not. And unlike Lake Retba, if you fill a glass from Lake Hillier, the water will retain its color. You probably shouldn't drink it, though.

CAVE OF THE CRYSTALS

IN NAICA, MEXICO, THERE ARE SELENITE CRYSTALS AS LARGE as twelve meters long, weighing as much as fifty-five tons. Naica rests atop an underground magma chamber, and intense amounts of heat and pressure have formed the crystals there over the past 500,000 years. Until the year 2000, the cave was flooded with water and unexplored. Silver, zinc, and lead miners in Naica found and drained the cave and its nearby sisters, which include the Cave of Swords, containing smaller, sharper crystals, and the Ice Palace, which is filled with even smaller, threadlike crystals.

Selenite, a variety of the mineral gypsum, is very soft, so soft that it can be scratched with a fingernail. These giant selenite crystals are used to being in water, and they are now deteriorating in the hot, dry air, so scientists are studying the cave as quickly as possible. The cave will likely be filled with water again as soon as the nearby silver and lead mines are exhausted. In order to bear the heat—which can rise to a debilitating 136 degrees in the caves—scientists must wear refrigerated suits, but the cooling period only lasts for half an hour at a time, so it's difficult to get any real work done. For quite some time, researchers were unable to find any sort of organic matter in the cave, but in 2017 scientists were able to extract and reanimate bacteria embedded in some of the crystals; the bacteria are not closely related, genetically, to any other known species.

SEA OF STARS

AT JUST THE RIGHT TIME OF YEAR, UNDER THE RIGHT CONDITIONS, stars in the sea mirror those in the sky above.

Bioluminescent creatures can be found throughout the Pacific and Atlantic Oceans, but rarely so spectacularly as on Vaadhoo Island in the Maldives. Dinoflagellates, a specific type of phytoplankton, float in on the tides, and during the day are a rusty red. But at night, when they are disturbed by the rocking of the waves, they activate a protein called luciferase—and they glow. You can see each individual organism emitting its own light, with trails of glowing blue flowing behind them.

Unlike fireflies or other bioluminescent creatures on land, dinoflagellates are not attempting to attract a mate. They are trying to warn off predators, for while their glow draws attention, they will *continue* to glow once eaten, making them a dangerous snack. They also produce toxins, so as tempting as it might be to swim beneath and among the stars, it's a sight best enjoyed from shore.

IN SEARCH OF MAGIC

You can create your own little sea of stars . . . Dinoflagellates, like most other things, are available online! You can observe their circadian rhythms as they follow their own night and day (which may or may not mirror reality in this kind of setting) and experiment with what stimulates their luciferase . . . and what allows them to be at rest. Similarly, glowworms are available for sale at some fishing outlets.

You can also create your own "quicksand" (see page 52) by mixing ¾ cup of water with one cup of cornstarch. The mixture will behave much the same way quicksand does, and you can experiment with the state that exists between solid and liquid.

TIANZI MOUNTAIN

THE QUARTZ SANDSTONE PEAKS OF the Tianzi Mountain in China rise as high as 4,000 feet above sea level, but can be as narrow as 1,500 feet at the base. Two of the peaks of Tianzi are separated by only a meter, and some brave souls jump across the chasm between them. Others choose to cross the natural Bridge of Immortality, a tree-covered arch thousands of feet above the ground.

Weathered by millennia after the seas of the Himalayas drained, these peaks inspire legends, some of which are based in truth. In 1353, the Tujia ethnic group revolted against the Great Yuan, the reigning dynasty of that time. The Tujia leader, crowned King Xiang, or Son of Heaven, set up a new kingdom in the mountain. But thirty years later Emperor Zhu Yuanzhang laid siege, and King Xiang fell to his death at the mountain's base. Several of the peaks are said to be King Xiang's soldiers, his horse, and his lover. Shentang Gulf, which swallowed King Xiang, is essentially untouched. The only way down is a nine-step natural ladder, so small that only one foot can step at a time—and at the bottom of the basin is a dark, mysterious pool.

MONT SAINT-MICHEL

WHILE THE CASTLE OF MONT SAINT-MICHEL IS CERTAINLY NOT a product of nature, it is beautiful. Built on a tiny island off of Normandy, France, this near-circular abbey was a battle stronghold, the tides and wide coastal flats of its surroundings making it easily defensible—so much so that it was never conquered during the Hundred Years' War.

Those tides produce some strange and rather terrifying effects, however. Varying in height by as much as fifty feet and moving at a speed of twelve miles per hour, the tides can produce a mini-wave so large and long-lasting that it is surfable. The tides also produce extreme quicksand conditions. When saturated loose sand is agitated—as when someone walks across it—and the water in the sand has nowhere to go, it creates a liquefied soil that cannot support weight or movement. In the Middle Ages, knights on horseback sank into the sand never to be found again—and these perils are still there today. If you decide to skip the causeway and walk across the tidal flats, you should do so with a tour group. You will find yourself sinking up to your knee, going deeper the more you move, though you probably won't go further than your hips. But if you remain trapped by the sand when the tide comes in, you will drown.

SALAR DE UYUNI

WITH AN ELEVATION SHIFT OF ONLY THREE FEET IN AN AREA of 4,000 square miles, the salt flats of Bolivia are just about the flattest place on Earth. The flats were formed when prehistoric lakes dried, and the fossilized remains of coral and algae can be found in the islands at the center. The brine beneath the salt crust contains 60 percent of the world's known lithium reserves, and of course the flats are mined for salt, as well. Some have even gone so far as to build hotels out of bricks of salt, though these are actually not sustainable as they drain the area's already poor water resources.

There are two seasons in Salar de Uyuni. In the dry season, the salt crusts over and cracks, allowing visitors to see the alternating layers of brine and solidified salt. But in the rainy season, a layer of water rests atop the salt flats, forming the world's largest mirror. When the light is right, it is impossible to distinguish the sky from the earth, as the horizon folds in on itself. The light at sunrise and sunset gives a sense that you are standing in a sea of fire.

GORËME

THE TOWN OF GORËME IN CAPPADOCIA,
Turkey, is home to the oddest of rock structures.
Pointy little stone houses and even towering
mountain-like stone apartment buildings carved
with windows and doors look like something out
of a strange fairy village.

Indeed, these structures are nicknamed "fairy
chimneys," and they were formed by a combi-
nation of nature and human craftsmanship. An
ancient volcanic eruption left behind mountains of
ash, which consolidated over the years into a soft,
porous rock called tuff and combined with the
regular volcanic rock, basalt. Erosion took care of
the rest, leaving behind these pointy or sometimes
mushroom-shaped towers.

Centuries ago, the fairy chimneys served as a
refuge. Persecuted Christians fleeing the Roman
Empire dug a honeycomb-like network of homes,
churches, and even stables into the soft rock. They
also bored down into the rock, hiding up to ten
thousand people when necessary.

Today, you can find the remnants of hidden
air vents, see the blackened ceilings in caves used
as kitchens, and even stay in a cave hotel, which
is probably somewhat more comfortable than the
original dwellings were.

TO SUA TRENCH

TO SUA, IN SAMOA, LITERALLY TRANSLATES TO "BIG HOLE"— and indeed it is. At around ninety feet deep, a free-fall dive here is exhilarating but safe—at high tide, at least. The water depth varies because this is no ordinary lake—it is tide-fed, crystalline seawater, filled with tropical fish and gentle sand.

The activity of the Lotofaga volcano (now extinct) and subsequent years of erosion left the area around To Sua filled with underground canals that feed the trench. These canals also produce blowholes, which are shafts in the ground leading to the ocean below. When a large enough wave comes, water rushes in and shoots up these shafts in a powerful blast—much like a whale's blowhole. Essentially, To Sua is an extremely large blowhole that never empties.

There are two ways to get into To Sua: the aforementioned dive or a somewhat slippery but still sturdy ladder. Once you get down into the trench, there is a platform that you can rest on as well as jump on and off of, and if you swim to the western wall, you'll even find a small, sandy beach—assuming the tide is low enough.

CROOKED FOREST

THE PINE TREES IN POLAND'S KRZYWY LAS, OR CROOKED FOREST, grow in a strange J-shape, hovering just inches above the ground for a span of three to nine feet, before beginning to reach for the sky. Each horizontal angle points directly to the north. There are only 400 or so crooked trees, and the surrounding forest grows normally. They appear to have been planted around 1930, and the theories for their existence range from the unlikely to the *very* unlikely.

One guess is that a strong gravitational pull kept the trees growing sideways for a time . . . which isn't really how gravity works. Another posits that a heavy snowfall stunted the trees' growth . . . but that would have been a *very* targeted snowfall, since the surrounding trees are fine. Panzers might have plowed some of the trees over during WWII . . . but in a circle, not to create a path? The most likely explanation is that the trees were formed this way intentionally, like really, really big bonsai, creating a natural angle that could then be used in shipbuilding or some other application for curved timber.

But no one really knows, because whether the cause was German tanks or snow, WWII interrupted whatever was going on, and no one who remembers is alive to tell the tale.

WAITOMO

THERE ARE STARS UNDERGROUND.
In the limestone Waitomo Caves of New Zealand, glowworms hang from the ceiling, floating above the underground river. *Arachnocampa luminosa*, a species found only in New Zealand, looks like a dripping star. The caves are lit only by its glow, and at first your mind interprets what you are seeing as the sky above. But as your eyes adjust, it becomes clear that the ceiling of the cave is very close and these stars edge their way toward you. It is a miraculous sight.

Arachnocampa luminosa are not actually worms, but the larvae of a mosquito-like fly. They are maggots, and in the light they look like it. The glow is caused by luciferase, the same chemical that phytoplankton produce, but the glowworm has a more predatory and less protective intention. The larvae secrete strings of silk fibers and build tubes into which they insert themselves, then they produce sticky globules of glowing mucus that hang like pearls on the fibers. These globules attract small insects, which get stuck in the mucus and feed the larvae.

It is perhaps better to leave the lights off.

THE DOOR TO HELL

ANY ACTIVE VOLCANIC CRATER FILLED WITH A LAVA LAKE, from Kīlauea in Hawai'i to Nyiragongo in the Democratic Republic of the Congo, could be called the Door to Hell. But because Darvaza Gas Crater in Turkmenistan is man-made, it is particularly terrifying.

No one knows *for sure* what happened, because there are no records. But the widely accepted explanation is that in 1971, a team of Soviet scientists began drilling for oil in Turkmenistan. They struck a pocket of natural gas, and their rig

fell into the crater it formed. Fearing the spread of methane, which, while non-toxic, displaces oxygen and would cause the surrounding wildlife to die, they set the pit on fire. And it is still burning.

The crater is 225 feet wide and 90 feet deep . . . and the government is now marketing it as a tourist destination. If they are able to gain entry to the country, visitors can camp around the pit, keeping warm during the freezing desert night. The crater is *very* hot, and though the methane is burning, there is still so much of it that the oxygen levels around the crater are lower than average, making it difficult to breathe. From time to time, spiders lured by the bright light and heat surge into the pit by the thousands and burn.

HAUNTED PLACES

THERE ARE SOME PRETTY CREEPY PLACES IN THE WORLD. AND *some of them have documented histories. Places like Chernobyl, Auschwitz, or Alcatraz, sites of grisly murders or insane asylums—these places aren't magical, they're tragic, and we're not going to explore them here.*

Frankly, some of the sites we are going to explore are equally tragic. Terrible things happened in Salem, New Orleans, and many other places, and no amount of time can diminish that. But enough time has passed that some of these events have become legend and taken on a kind of dark magic.

Hauntings, sightings, strange happenings, and general icky feelings permeate certain places on Earth. Often when you're exploring the world, you can just tell, even without any knowledge whatsoever of your surroundings, that something bad is—or was—there. And there is often a historical reason for that feeling . . . but sometimes there isn't. Sometimes, a story is all there is—and that's enough.

PANTÉON DE BELÉN

THE PANTÉON DE BELÉN IN GUADALAJARA IS ONE OF THE MOST architecturally gorgeous cemeteries in all the world . . . and it's *superhaunted*. This cemetery was built in 1848 and only in use for fifty years, but it is home to not just ghosts, but pirates, hounds, and many more creatures of the night— including a vampire.

In the 1930s, Guadalajara was in a state of terror. Supposedly, residents were finding the bodies of their pets drained of blood, and some say there were even child victims. A group of vigilantes staked out the graveyard, where they found a pale figure feasting on his most recent body. Having boned up on their Bram Stoker beforehand, they pinned their villain to the ground and thrust a stake into his heart. The men buried the creature, stake intact, and covered his grave in concrete. But that was not quite the end of the vampire of Pantéon de Belén. The stake left in his heart sprouted, pushed up through the concrete slab covering, and grew into an enormous tree. If you cut its branches, blood, not sap, seeps out from the wound. The faces of the vampire's victims can be seen in its bark. The tree is cared for, watered, and fed to appease the vampire so that he will never return.

BALLYBOLEY FOREST

BALLYBOLEY FOREST IN NORTHERN IRELAND IS A BEAUTIFUL and seemingly innocuous woodland. There is evidence that it was a site of Druidic rituals, though that doesn't necessarily imply anything sinister. But Ballyboley does have a frightening past. In the fifteenth, sixteenth, and seventeenth centuries, there are accounts of people from the surrounding villages disappearing into the forest.

Legends of spirits and hauntings persist from that time, with one in particular standing out: in 1997, it was reported that two men went into the forest and heard strange sounds—flapping, a woman moaning. They left the path to follow the sound and came upon a grove of trees smeared with blood. The flapping sounds surrounded them, and they fled in terror. As the men ran, they looked back and saw four figures clad in brown rags, watching them go.

Today, there are widespread reports of general creepy feelings, as the forest is rumored to be a gateway to the "Otherworld." It is said that locals will not venture into the forest, for fear of what lives there.

THE PARIS CATACOMBS

THE REMAINS OF SIX MILLION PEOPLE FILL THE CATACOMBS beneath Paris.

By the eighteenth century, after a number of plagues, the densely populated City of Light was beginning to overflow with corpses. The cemetery of Les Innocents in particular, which was situated on the swampy right bank of the Seine, was so full that the masses of bodies were collapsing the basement walls of the surrounding buildings.

But the left bank of the Seine was formed by much firmer ground. It was, in fact, not just stable, but also riddled with tunnels from an abandoned limestone mine. (Much of the city is built from this same limestone.) And so over the course of two years, wagons covered in black cloth and escorted by priests ferried skeletons from the cemeteries of Paris to this new ossuary.

At first, the new repository was just a jumble of bones. Certainly no one could identify who was who at this point. But Louis-Étienne Héricart de Thury, the director of the Paris Mine Inspection Service and therefore pretty much in charge of the situation, had an artistic, if macabre, eye. He sorted the skulls and femurs, stacking and lining the walls of the catacombs with them. He set aside skeletal deformities to put in a separate room. He arranged the bones into elaborate mosaics and carved various inscriptions into the walls.

Above the entrance, he carved the phrase: "Halt, this is the realm of death." It is, indeed.

SALEM

WE ALL KNOW THE BASIC STORY OF SALEM, MASSACHUSETTS, and it's not a good one. In a profound case of mass hysteria, twenty people—fourteen of whom were women—were executed in 1692 on charges of witchcraft. Others, including children, died in prison.

The first to die, on June 10, 1692, was Bridget Bishop. Bishop, a widow, didn't dress according to Puritan standards, was rumored to run a tavern in her home, and was generally outspoken and "immoral." The Lyceum Bar and Grill now stands where her orchard had been, and her ghost has been seen looking out its windows.

After a short break to consider whether this was the right thing to do, the hangings resumed. On July 16, 1692, five more women were executed, including Sarah Good, a homeless beggar. Sarah's story is a particularly sad one—her estranged husband testified against her, as did her frightened five-year-old daughter. Sarah was pregnant at the time of her trial, and so her execution was stayed until after the birth—but she was given no food and no bedding, and the baby died within days. Just before she went to the gallows, Sarah was visited by Reverend Noyes, presumably to see if he could save her soul before death. She told him, "God will give you blood to drink." Her curse took some time to bear

fruit, but twenty-five years later, the reverend had an aneurysm and blood filled his lungs and throat as he died.

But the most profound curse came from Giles Corey. Corey was a local farmer and upstanding member of the church, but by this point the witch-hunting hysteria had grown so fevered that this counted for naught. Many of the accused confessed—because they were tortured into doing so. But Giles Corey refused. After days of enduring *peine forte et dure*, a method of torture that involved placing a plank atop a prone body and piling increasingly heavy stones on it, Corey died. His last words were, "I curse you and Salem." Four years later, his tormenter died of a heart attack, and Corey's ghost can still be seen lurking in the town's graveyards—frequently as a warning that disaster is about to strike Salem.

By 1982, the town of Salem had embraced its tragic and spooky past. Salem Haunted Happenings Festival is a family-friendly event celebrated every October, with Wiccan rituals, costume balls, ghost tours, and more. Over 250,000 visitors per year attend this festival at the self-proclaimed "haunted capital of the world."

IN SEARCH OF MAGIC

Almost every town has a haunted house, and every culture in the world has its demons and devils. These days, it can be hard to imagine ordinary folks sitting around telling stories of hauntings or demons, much less actually believing in them, but you might be surprised. Even if most of us don't believe in ghosts, we probably still won't want to set foot in that creepy house that everybody says is haunted, and there are still plenty of people who hold their breath every time they pass a graveyard.

Without breaking any laws or putting yourself in danger, consider testing your limits a little bit! Host a séance with a gathering of like-minded friends, perhaps even inviting a professional medium. If you're really brave, you could see if you can conjure a demon. Just make sure you've put all the necessary safeguards in place first, including but not limited to a salt circle, some protective crystals, and a pentagram.

DAVELIS CAVE

DAVELIS CAVE IS LOCATED ON, OR RATHER IN, THE
Pendeli Mountain in Greece. Carved into the mountain is a Byz-
antine church, with half dedicated to St. Spyridon, and the other,
to St. Nicholas. In the twelfth century, hermit monks worshipped
there. But deeper in the cave are signs that this was also a place of
worship for an even earlier god—Pan, the goat-legged god of the
wild. And yet, the cave is named after a much more recent dwell-
er—a nineteenth-century highwayman named Davelis, who used
the cave as his hideout.

Up until that point in history, the cave was relatively quiet,
paranormally speaking. But since Davelis's death, there have been
numerous reports of a wide variety of strange happenings in the
vicinity, from glowing orbs and human-shaped figures of mist to
disappearing and reappearing creatures that look like a twisted
version of sheep.

After some government excavation in the 1980s (a project that was secretive in nature and shut down abruptly, leaving
equipment behind), things got even weirder. Fresh, wet cement
showed footprints walking up to a cave wall and stopping, with no
evidence of where the walker went from there—perhaps through
the rock? Empty cars have been known to roll uphill near the cave's
entrance, and cameras sometimes stop working or produce pic-
tures of forms that the photographer never saw.

The depths of the cave have been explored by various paranormal enthusiasts, but very little has been reported, frequently
because the explorers, despite being professionals, either come
back disoriented or don't come back at all. All of this has brought
Davelis Cave some cachet in certain unsavory circles; from time to
time, the remnants of animal sacrifices and other occult activities
are left behind in its depths to be found by curious tourists.

ISLAND OF THE DOLLS

ISLA DE LAS MUÑECAS IS A MAN-MADE FLOATING GARDEN JUST south of Mexico City. It's a tiny island set between the canals of Xochimilco, the ancient aqueduct system, and it has a tragic history. Over fifty years ago, Don Julian Santana Barrera, the caretaker of the island, found the body of a drowned little girl. Days later, when a doll washed ashore, Barrera believed it belonged to the girl and hung it on a tree to honor her.

But as time went on, Barrera became convinced he was being haunted and hung doll after doll on the trees and in the grasses; he claimed that each doll was possessed by a dead little girl, and he was attempting to appease their spirits. He continued adding to the collection of dolls, searching for unwanted toys in both the canal and in rubbish dumps until the end of his life. His body was eventually found, drowned, in the same place where he had come upon the little girl.

Whatever Barrera's intentions, the result is a nightmarish collection of staring, dead-eyed dolls, many of which are missing limbs and some of which are painted red to resemble blood. While locals believe that Isla de las Muñecas is charmed, it has become a destination for those curious about the macabre. Barrera's descendants run the island as a tourist destination, and visitors add new dolls every year.

Some sources have questioned whether the little girl in question ever existed or Barrera invented her in his loneliness and solitude. If that is the case, it is simply another kind of tragedy.

DEVIL'S GATE DAM

THERE'S ROCK THAT LOOKS LIKE THE DEVIL IN PASADENA, California. The attached dam, built adjacent to the stone in 1920, harnesses the Arroyo Seco, a river that the Tongva Native American tribe says laughs with the sound of the trickster god Coyote.

While the Arroyo Seco hasn't flooded in some time, it has drawn the attention of some famous paranormal enthusiasts, including L. Ron Hubbard, founder of Scientology, as well as Jack Parsons, founder of the nearby Jet Propulsion Lab. Believing the rock to be a literal hellmouth, Parsons, Hubbard, and other members of their occult society met at the dam at night to perform rituals intended to conceive a "moonchild," a higher and more powerful version of man. As far as we know, they were unsuccessful, and Parsons died in an explosion not long after their excursions.

Today, residents avoid the dam, despite the inviting nature of the surrounding wooded area. Those who do go near it report feelings of dread, terror, and occasionally report sightings of demons, ghosts, and other beings likely to lurk around a hellmouth.

CANNOCK CHASE

THERE ARE MONSTERS IN THE WOODS of Cannock Chase, part of the countryside in Staffordshire, England. There have been sightings of UFOs, ghosts, and a number of strange animals. In 2003 there were reports of a crocodile—or at least some sort of large, green serpentine creature—dwelling in a nearby pond. Since the late 1960s, up to the present day, there have been dozens of reports of large, almost panther-sized black cats roaming through the forest, particularly in the cemetery within its depths—a burial site which oddly houses hundreds of German soldiers who died in WWI and WWII.

These days, there is something a lot scarier than cats lurking in the forest. In April 2007, the local *Stafford Post* newspaper reported on a "rash" of werewolf sightings in the area. In that same cemetery, locals reported seeing large dogs rise up on their hind legs, standing six or seven feet tall, and run away upright. The remains of mutilated deer and other animals have also been found in the woods.

POVEGLIA

POVEGLIA IS ACTUALLY TWO ISLANDS, LOCATED BETWEEN Venice and Lido, and it has a fairly awful history. In the late 1700s it was a place of quarantine for plague victims and lepers, and then later for victims of mental illness. An asylum for the mentally ill was supposedly built in 1922, though reports of its existence vary. Apparently, the presiding doctor practiced crude lobotomies and other experimental procedures on his patients; they got their revenge, however, as legend says that he jumped to his death from the hospital tower, claiming their ghosts were driving him as mad as his patients.

It is believed that between the plague, leprosy, and deaths at the mental asylum, there are as many as 160,000 bodies buried on these tiny islands, and it is said that so many were burned during the plague that the soil is 50 percent ash. The islands are now completely abandoned, and the structures left standing are overgrown. In a place with astronomically high property values and a booming tourist scene, Poveglia is somehow left completely alone.

BELL WITCH CAVE

PERHAPS THE MOST FAMOUS HAUNTING IN NORTH AMERICA occurred in the early 1800s in Adams, Tennessee. John Bell and his family were tormented for years by a ghost they named "Kate." The Bell family often found strange, mismatched animals in their cornfield, and sometimes they were awakened in the night by loud, banging noises or by being stripped of their blankets while sleeping. Word spread, so widely that Andrew Jackson, then serving in the U.S. Army, came to the farm intent on meeting and hopefully defeating this sinister woman . . . but he and his men failed and fled the scene.

Betsy Bell, the youngest of the family, suffered slaps and scratches from invisible hands that nevertheless would leave welts across her face. Kate spent years threatening to kill John Bell, tripping him as he walked, slapping him, and apparently giving him some kind of malady that caused his face to twitch and made it difficult to swallow. In 1820, three years after Kate's first appearance, she poisoned John Bell. Not long after, Betsy became engaged, but Kate did not approve of the match, and tormented Betsy day and night until she finally broke off the relationship in 1821.

That seemed to satisfy Kate at last, and she left the family alone for seven years. She returned in 1828 and spoke only with John Bell Jr., intimating that there had been a purpose to everything she did, though she never said what it was. She claimed that she would return 107 years later, but by 1935 the family had understandably gone elsewhere.

The original farmhouse is now gone, but a replica has been built and tours are available. Beneath the earth is a cave, estimated to be fifteen feet deep, that is said to be where Kate now makes her home.

BHANGARH RUINS

BHANGARH FORT IN INDIA IS TECHNICALLY A SMALL CITY, BUILT in the sixteenth century by Maharajah Bhagwant Das for his general Raja Man Singh—but today it is in ruins. The official reason for this state of disrepair is that there was a terrible famine in the seventeenth century, but hardly anybody believes that.

There are two legends explaining its emptiness. The first features a holy man named Baba Balau Nath. His house apparently stood above the rest—and he wanted it to remain that way. He warned that should any building reach nearer the sky than his own, casting a shadow over him, he would destroy the city. One of the later rulers of Bhangarh did build columns that cast such a shadow—and look what happened.

The second legend tells of a dark wizard, Singhia Sevra, who fell in unrequited love with Ratnavati, Bhangarh's princess. When Ratnavati went shopping for ittar, a perfume, the wizard attempted to replace it with a love potion. But Ratnavati saw through him and tossed the potion at a boulder. This action dislodged the boulder, and it rolled down the mountainside, crushing the wizard. As he lay dying, he cursed Bhangarh and predicted that the fort would soon be destroyed. Shortly thereafter, Bhangarh was invaded by the Ajabgarh—marauders from the north—and all 10,000 residents were killed, including the princess.

The fort was never repopulated, and rumors of paranormal activity soon began. Eerie music can be heard at night, and there are said to be any number of ghosts haunting the city, including Balau Nath, Sevra, and Ratnavati. Visitors often disappear or are injured or even killed while traveling to and from Bhangarh. It is a place of such concern, in fact, that the Indian government has forbidden entry to the fort after sunset and before sunrise.

DUDLEY CASTLE

DUDLEY CASTLE IS SAID TO BE THE MOST HAUNTED CASTLE in England—and there's a lot of competition. Built in 1130, it is home to at least three separate ghosts, partly due to the sheer number of deaths, wars, and other events the castle has withstood.

The ancient chapel undercroft is haunted by the ghost of Baron John de Somery, who was apparently among the crueler lords of the castle. Perhaps it is his body that rests in the stone coffin at the center of the undercroft—no one knows for certain. Visitors have seen feet standing near the casket and have felt hands tugging at the clothes, shoving them, or prodding them.

Careful observers will also often hear the echoes of a drum and the rousing calls of a march to battle. This ghost is said to be that of a little boy, felled by a single shot in the mid-seventeenth century, during the English Civil War. This was an unlikely, and therefore especially unfortunate way to die, since the seventeenth-century musket was apparently the least accurate gun ever made.

But the most famous of Dudley's ghosts is the Grey Lady. There are many Grey Ladies all over the world; this one is said to be the ghost of Dorothy Beaumont. Her husband was second-in-command of the Royalist forces during the English Civil War, and they were briefly quartered at Dudley Castle. Dorothy gave birth during their stay, but as happened so often, the infant died in childbirth and she herself passed shortly thereafter. On her deathbed, Dorothy asked to be buried beside her daughter and for her husband to attend her funeral. Neither request ended up being granted, and she now haunts the halls of Dudley Castle, as well as the nearby tavern named after her. Photographs of her were captured as recently as 2014.

MA-NO UMI

WE'RE ALL FAMILIAR WITH THE BERMUDA TRIANGLE. BUT THERE
is a similar, less widely known but perhaps more dangerous, location known as
Ma-no Umi, which translates to "The Devil's Sea." A vortex in the Pacific Ocean
about sixty miles south of Tokyo, Ma-no Umi has spawned numerous legends of
sea dragons, aliens, and the vanished remains of countless ships. Kublai Khan, the
Mongolian warlord of the thirteenth century, is said to have tried twice to sail his
fleet across its waters to attack Japan, but both times he lost everything, with
death tolls supposedly nearing 150,000 men. Divers and marine archaeologists
have found the remains of some of these ships.

Like the Bermuda Triangle, Ma-no Umi's powers are not limited to the water.
In 1971, pilot Takeo Tada saw what appeared to be an orange flying saucer above the
Devil's Sea. He watched it for some time, until it rose up above the clouds and disappeared. Sixteen years later, pilot Tetsuzan Naito's instruments seized up without
warning as his plane was engulfed in an eerie green fog that swallowed all sound.

But the majority of stories about Ma-no Umi come from World War II, starting with a Japanese pilot who claimed to have seen a giant serpent swimming in
the waters beneath him. As the war raged, Japanese warships, and of course a
number of fishing vessels, traveled across the Devil's Sea, but were lost, apparently without cause. Japan sent a research vessel to investigate, but it too met
its fate. When the wreck of research vessel *Kaio Maru 5* was found, its crew was
missing. The Japanese government elected to cease all research in the area and
declared Ma-no Umi unsafe.

THE PINE BARRENS

IN A STATE RENOWNED FOR ITS LACK OF BEAUTY, THE SWAMPY, forested Pine Barrens of New Jersey can be hauntingly lovely—with *haunting* being the operative word. On the HBO show *The Sopranos*, the Pine Barrens made for an ideal place to dump a body, because nobody goes too far into the woods. The Pine Barrens are said to be home to any number of spirits and ghouls—most famously, the Jersey Devil.

The Jersey Devil is said to have been born to Deborah Leeds in 1735. A resident of the Pine Barrens, Mother Leeds was pregnant for the thirteenth time, and she had had enough. She asked God to "let this one be a devil." When the baby boy was born months later, he appeared normal—at least at first. But shortly after his birth, the baby began growing at an alarming rate, sprouting horns and claws and bat-like wings. His eyes glowed red, and he savaged anyone he could reach, including the midwife, his father, and some of his siblings.

The Devil has terrorized the surrounding area ever since. Joseph Bonaparte, older brother of Napoleon, tried to hunt him down in 1820. In 1909 strange footprints led to a statewide hunt. Bloodhounds refused to follow the tracks, and schools and mills in the surrounding area were closed because residents refused to leave their homes. The Devil was spotted in towns across the state, described as a twisted creature with the head of a horse, the legs of a goat, and wings. Officers in Camden fired upon it to no avail. It hasn't caused such widespread panic since, but the Jersey Devil is still seen in the Pine Barrens to this day.

The Jersey Devil has a softer side, at least toward his fellow Pine Barrens residents. The Devil shares his hunting grounds with Captain Kidd, and the two can often be seen walking together—but Kidd is without his head, having had his neck stretched back in London in 1701. The Devil also sits and stares out at the water with the Golden-Haired Girl, as she holds her vigil for her lover lost at sea. The Black Doctor, the spirit of African American James Still who practiced medicine despite laws preventing him from doing so, aids injured or stranded travelers in the Pine Barrens, and a White Stag helps those who are lost find their way home.

NEW ORLEANS

CALLED THE MOST HAUNTED CITY IN AMERICA, NEW ORLEANS is teeming with ghosts and haunted houses, and there are more ghost tours than regular historical ones. The city's past as the center of the slave trade makes its hauntings particularly grim, as do the natural disasters of the more recent past. Some of the eeriest places include abandoned hospitals and amusement parks, empty since Hurricane Katrina. Other haunted locations have been filled with actors and props, and in some cases a blood donation will serve as your entry fee.

The most famous, and one of the most horrifying, haunted houses in New Orleans is the LaLaurie Mansion. In 1833, Madame LaLaurie had been ordered to set her slaves free after a household slave died under suspicious circumstances—but, one by one, she brought them all back. And then, a year later, a fire in the house revealed seven slaves who had been kept chained. They had been starved and, rumor has it, tortured and experimented on. This so enraged the people of New Orleans that they set upon the house as a mob, ripping it down to the studs. Madame LaLaurie escaped unharmed. However, her spirit seems to have returned to the house, as reports of violence continued. In 1894, a tenant was found murdered; in the days and weeks before, he had been raving about a demon in the house that would not rest until he was dead. In the late 1800s the house also served as a boarding school for girls—and these girls would approach their teachers, sobbing, displaying deep gouges in their arms. "That woman did it," they said. Since Madame LaLaurie, no one has retained ownership of the house for more than five years—financial troubles or creepy happenings always drive them out.

The cemeteries of New Orleans are all said to be haunted as well, but the oldest and most famous is St. Louis Cemetery No. 1. A tiny burial site spanning only one block, it is a warren holding 100,000 bodies and counting, as it is still active. Marie Laveau, the Voodoo Queen of New Orleans, was laid to rest there. Marie's father was a free black man, while her mother was a free woman of Native American, African, and French descent. Marie appears to have followed her mother's tradition of fortune-telling and working with herbal remedies, but took it much further, incorporating Voodoo practices with Roman Catholic saints and prayers. Marie was at the height of her popularity in the 1830s, when she held rituals in Congo Square, the place where free and enslaved blacks could congregate freely. She also held annual ceremonies on St. John's Eve at Lake Pontchartrain, which were attended by thousands of people—black and white. Her eerie knowledge of the goings on of New Orleans society made her the most sought-after (and the most feared) Voodoo practitioner in the city. Whether her vast knowledge came from her power as a brothel owner, her work as a hairdresser, her network within the slave community, or her occult practices remains a mystery. These days, Marie Laveau's spirit is most frequently found roaming the Quarter, but legend has it that marking her grave with three X's and leaving a gift will induce her to grant your wish. This legend was so popular that Laveau's grave was defaced, leading to the closure of St. Louis Cemetery No. 1 to the public in 2015.

There are dozens more stories and haunted locations in this city filled with Cities of the Dead.

THE PAST IN THE PRESENT

THERE ARE PLACES IN THE WORLD WHERE TIME FEELS AS THOUGH *it has* stopped, *where certain rituals and traditions that seem almost impossible to maintain in this world of Google and strip malls just . . . carry on. This honoring of old gods, of magic, of ghosts and demons and fairies is a profound testament to the importance of our roots.*

Some of these rituals and locations are familiar worldwide, like the Day of the Dead celebration in Mexico. But others might be less widely known, like Famadihana in Madagascar or Ásatrúarfélagið in Reykjavik. Some are reflective of true religions, while others are a way of celebrating what has gone before. But for the most part, they are practiced in much the same manner as they always have been. In this way, these traditions are different from the pagan holiday Ostara's conversion to Easter, though some of Ostara's practices (like coloring eggs) are still part of the holiday.

Most of the practices honored in this chapter date back hundreds, if not thousands, of years. And for the most part, they are not declining but growing in popularity, as more and more people are finding faith, peace, and joy in what once was and is still.

REYKJAVIK

THOSE OF US WHO HAVE BEEN ENJOYING THE *THOR* MOVIES and Neil Gaiman's *American Gods* might be delighted to know that worship of Norse gods is on the rise. Ásatrúarfélagið, meaning "Ásatrú Fellowship," is the modern version of Ásatrú, the ancient religion of the Vikings. It was launched (or relaunched) on the summer solstice in 1972. Ásatrúarfélagið is an official religion, collecting tithes and performing wedding ceremonies, conducting name-giving and coming-of-age rituals as well as burials on its own burial ground.

Membership started off very low (not even a hundred people), but has skyrocketed in recent years, and it is now the sixth-largest religion in Iceland. Jónsmessa, or Midsummer, features a Norse version of selkies, talking cows, and seductive elves, and in 1973 the first public *blót* or ritual sacrifice was made to an effigy of Thor. This practice was officially outlawed in Iceland around the year 1000 in favor of Christianity, though it is likely that Ásatrú never fully died out, remaining secret for over a thousand years.

Like Western European paganism, modern Ásatrú practice doesn't rely too much on official dogma. Odin, Thor, Freyja, Frigg, Loki, and many, many other traditional gods are not specifically worshipped—though that definition may vary from person to person—but instead are used as symbols and parables to define a way of life. Norse gods are notably imperfect and considered more as nonjudgmental friends and examples. While in the past, Ásatrú may have been fairly violent and male-dominated, the current practice is one of ease with nature and the forces of good. It seeks to be a gender-equal religion of peace and tolerance.

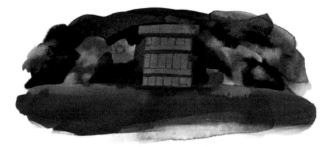

HAFNARFJÖRÒUR

WHILE BELIEF IN THOR AND ODIN IS LIMITED TO A FEW FAITHFUL, more than half the people in Iceland believe in elves. Huldufólk, or the Secret Folk, as they are known, live across the entire island, but are said to concentrate in Hafnarfjöròur, a harbor town just outside Reykjavik.

For the people of Iceland, the existence of elves is simply a matter of course. Roads are diverted in order to avoid volcanic rock formations that serve as churches for Huldufólk or hills that are their homes, and elf bonfires and dances are held on Thirteenth Night (January 6). Huldufólk are not the otherworldly beautiful beings of J.R.R. Tolkien or Robert Kirk mythology; instead, they are small, humanlike creatures that live perfectly normal, nature-based lives. They farm, fish, have families, and, generally speaking, mind their own business.

When care is not taken with their dwellings, however, they will retaliate. Construction sites in Iceland that do not take into account the Huldufólk can expect mechanical failures, injuries, and, if they persist, even deaths. In 1970, the Icelandic Road and Coastal Administration had intended to blow up a series of rocks referred to locally as the Troll's Pass, but was convinced not to do so. The road remains uneven to this day, but as of 2013 there had been zero traffic accidents on it, as the grateful elves protect those who drive near their home. Similarly, in 2010 a man named Árni Johnsen was in a car accident in southwest Iceland, but remained miraculously uninjured. He believes he was saved by a family of elves known to dwell in a nearby boulder and actually had that thirty-ton boulder relocated to his home, after having consulted with the elves to make sure they would like to move to a place that had more fields and fewer cars.

GRAZ

AT LEAST AS TERRIFYING—AND AT LEAST AS MUCH FUN—AS American Halloween festivities, celebrations on Krampusnacht in Graz and other parts of Austria date back to long before Christ. Krampus is antlered and hairy, with cloven hoofs, a lolling tongue, and fangs. He likely has roots in both the traditional horned god of pagan religions as well as the Devil.

On the evening of December 5, Krampusnacht, the holiday's signature creature is said to roam villages searching for naughty children—the ones St. Nicholas won't be bothering with. He carries *ruten*, the birch switches used to beat those who were disobedient—and sometimes a child that falls in a gray area, behavior-wise, will be given the switches as a reminder to act better throughout the year. Krampus can be appeased with brandy . . . and maybe a ritual prayer.

Every Krampusnacht, parades of young men dressed as Krampus dance and jangle their way through villages and towns. Many of the costumes in these processions are unbelievably detailed and well made, worked from sheepskin and other natural materials and featuring hand-carved masks. They are handed down for generations. After the 1923 election in Austria, as part of the surge in fascism, Krampusnacht festivities were forbidden. They continued nonetheless, but remained so frowned upon that in the 1950s the government distributed pamphlets decrying Krampus as "an evil man." But toward the end of the twentieth century, Krampus came out of hiding and celebrating his night is now one of the most beloved rituals in Central European and Slavic countries.

TAIPEI

WEI-MING TEMPLE IN TAIPEI IS DEDICATED TO THE WORSHIP
of Hu Tianbao, the god of homosexuality. According to legend, Hu Tianbao was
a seventeenth-century soldier in love with an older official. He spied on the man
in the bathroom, and when caught, he confessed his feelings—and was beaten to
death for them. Later, he appeared to a man from his village in a dream, explaining the situation, and the man built a shrine in his honor.

Because homosexuals at the time were referred to using the slur "rabbits,"
Hu Tianbao became known as Tu'er Shen, the rabbit god. The shrine drew worshippers, and faith in Hu Tianbao grew, despite efforts of government suppres-
sion . . . that is, until the early twentieth century, toward the end of the Qing
dynasty, when worship of Hu Tianbao was forbidden outright.

But in 2005, Hu Tianbao made another visit, this time to a Taoist priest, who
erected Wei-ming Temple, the world's only shrine for homosexuals. Congre-
gants come in search of love, as Hu Tianbao acts in much the same way as Yu
Lao, the heterosexual matchmaker god. Worshippers write prayers, which are
then burned in ceremonial dedication and put out with rice wine. Others leave
offerings or take charms home to place under their pillows.

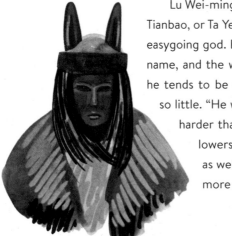

Lu Wei-ming, the temple's founder, describes Hu
Tianbao, or Ta Yeh as he prefers to call him, as a fairly
easygoing god. Because of the way he died, his nick-
name, and the way his followers have been treated,
he tends to be easily pleased, having been used to
so little. "He will be much more grateful and work
harder than other deities," Lu says. As his followers become less marginalized, Ta Yeh will
as well, and perhaps he will become a little
more demanding—as he should.

SAIDAI-JI TEMPLE

EVERY YEAR, ON THE THIRD SATURDAY IN THE MONTH OF
February, around 9,000 men gather at the Saidai-ji Temple in the Okayama Pre-
fecture of Japan. They dress only in loincloths, and they wrestle each other for a
pair of wooden sticks.

It's a glorious, joyful, and fun event that began 500 years ago. Every year,
priests at the temple would go through a New Year ascetic training—and at the
end, in February, they would receive paper talismans, called, *go-o*, symbolizing
their accomplishment. They would throw the talismans to the people, and anyone who received one would have good luck for the remainder of the year.

As the paper was delicate, it was replaced with sacred wooden *shingi*—and as
the demand was so high, it became a competition to see who could catch these
wooden sticks. In the hours before the priest throws the *shingi* from the temple
balcony, the mostly naked men gathered below are so full of excitement and
energy that even though it's freezing, they are often doused with water to keep
them cool and calm.

Shouting "Wasshoi! Wasshoi!" which loosely translates to "carry peace," the
men march toward the temple and scramble feverishly for the *shingi*. The man who
keeps hold of the sticks and places them in a *masu*, a wooden measuring box filled
with rice, is called the Lucky Man. He will be blessed with a year of happiness.

MADAGASCAR

EVERY FIVE TO SEVEN YEARS, THE Merina people of Madagascar practice a sacred ritual called Famidihana, or the turning of the bones. It's a celebration and an opportunity to honor, tend to, and literally dance with those we have lost. The Malagasy believe that until our bodies have completely decomposed, we remain partly in this world, able to influence and protect those we love.

Famidihana begins when an ancestor visits a living relative in a dream, asking for new clothes and warmth. The family consults an *ombiasy*—an astrologer—to determine the optimal moment to open the tomb. For a first Famidihana, the body is carried out feetfirst and brought to a crowd of raucously joyous family members, many of whom have traveled a long distance for the two-day celebration. The body is carefully rewrapped in a new silk shroud and raised overhead in a dance of reunion. By sunset, the body is returned to the tomb, now headfirst and facedown, to continue the process of moving into the next life. The tomb will not be reopened for another five to seven years, for the next family reunion/wake.

MARI EL REPUBLIC

IN THE WESTERN PART OF RUSSIA, ALONG THE VOLGA RIVER, is the Republic of Mari El, a secluded and insular community of Mari, an ethnic group with its own living language, some of whom practice the Mari religion. All along the Volga are sacred groves, small standing forests said to be filled with power. The Mari people worship in these groves, chanting and performing ritual sacrifices. Geese are consumed during religious festivals, as these are creatures that commune with the three elements of the sky, the earth, and the water. As part of the ritual, the geese are calmed with birch leaves before being sacrificed and prepared for a meal in the grove.

There are four different sects of the Mari religion, but all of them are extremely nature-based. They do have specific gods, or *jumo*, for each of the elements, though the pantheon can range to over 100. They include:

KUGU JUMO ◆ also called Kugurak, meaning "Elder," who serves as the foremost god. Many of the following gods are sometimes considered to be attributes or simply different faces of Kugu Jumo

TUL ◆ the god of fire

SURT ◆ the spirit of the household

SAKSA ◆ the god of fertility

KÜDRYRCHÖ JUMO ◆ the god of thunder

TUTYRA ◆ the god of fog

PURYSHO ◆ the god of fate, who creates the future of all humankind

AZYREN ◆ the god of death

SHUDYR-SHAMYCH ◆ the god of the stars

TYLMACHE ◆ the worker of the divine will

TYLZE ◆ the god of the moon

UZHARA ◆ the god of the dawn

MLANDE ◆ the god of earth

SHOCHYN-AVA ◆ the god of childbirth

TUNYA ◆ the god of the universe

Many of these gods have female counterparts: goddesses who serve as the feminine version of their unique power. Mari also believe in *keremets*, beings that are half-men, half-god. Some Mari view the *keremets* as evil tricksters or ghosts, while others treat them like a kind of guardian spirit.

The Mari way of life has been hard-won. Because of their beliefs, obviously logging is out, as is any work to do with water. For the most part, they farm and follow a lifestyle of communion with the natural world rarely to be found in modern times. Ivan the Terrible, in his bloody devotion to Christianity, attempted to force the Mari to convert, and during the Soviet era, the separation of ethnic groups was no longer really allowed, disempowering the Mari (among many other groups, like the Romuva of Lithuania). Today, Mari youth are streaming to Moscow and other cities, and the Mari people are working to preserve their culture as best they can.

MEXICO CITY

DÍA DE MUERTOS, THE MEXICAN CELEBRATION OF
those who have passed, has captured the imaginations of people all
over the world. As recently as the 1600s, it was observed toward
the end of summer, but gradually festivities have shifted to be in
line with Halloween, Samhain, All Saints' Day, and other holidays
associated with the dead that fall between October and November.

Día de Muertos can be traced back to Aztec festivals in honor
of the goddess Mictecacihuatl, the Queen of the Underworld,
who was sacrificed as an infant and always depicted as a gaping
skull. Rituals around Mictecacihuatl honoring deceased ancestors date back as many as 3,000 years and in some ways have
remained much the same.

Día de Muertos is not one day, but three. On midnight of the
first day, now celebrated on October 31, spirits of deceased children
are able to cross over and reunite with their families for a full day's
cycle. And on November 2 it is the adults' turn to cross. No matter
the age of the deceased when they passed, the crossing is thought
to be very difficult and tiring, and so families will build elaborate,
expensive *ofrendas*, or altars, decorated with candles, *cempasuchil*
(marigolds), fruit, turkey mole, and *pan de muerto*, bread baked specifically for the dead. The children will find toys and sugar skulls, and
adults have cigarettes and shots of mezcal awaiting them. As the
sun begins to set on November 2, the celebration moves out of the
home, as the entire community gathers at the cemetery, to tend to
gravestones, play music and cards, and dance.

This ritual can cost as much as two months' wages for a low-
income rural family, but these days spent honoring the ancestors
ensure that the living receive protection, good luck, and wisdom
throughout the rest of the year.

⇥ IN SEARCH OF MAGIC ⇤

This is a case where the line between appreciation and appropriation becomes thin. While it isn't likely that too many people outside of Madagascar would be tempted to practice Famadihana, there is so much that is appealing about celebrating Día de Muertos, worshipping Tu'er Shen, and caring for Huldufólk.

There are ways to appreciate these traditional practices without being in any way insensitive to the cultures they stem from. If you are not of Mexican descent, rather than hosting a Día de Muertos party, consider attending one, if you are welcome. Perhaps research the fair folk of your own indigenous culture, or at least the culture of the place you live, and find out what you can do for them.

And perhaps most importantly, consider living as the majority of these cultures still do or try to—as closely to nature as you can, with respect and even reverence for the world around you. If you're going to make an offering, share it with a god or being that feels in alignment with how you want to be in the world.

NIʻIHAU

THE LAST ISLAND IN THE HAWAIIAN CHAIN IS CALLED "The Forbidden Isle" for a reason. It is the only privately owned island in the state, having been sold by King Kamehameha V in 1864 to a woman named Elizabeth Sinclair for a whopping $10,000 (only about $135,000 today). Sinclair's descendants, the Robinsons, work very hard to protect the lifestyle of the island's 175-ish residents, keeping it as close to life in 1864 as possible, honoring a promise Sinclair made to the king.

Niʻihau has no paved roads or cars. There are no stores or restaurants—there aren't even police, doctors, a fire department—or indoor plumbing.

This is all 100 percent intentional. The island could have all of these things, but the Robinsons and the people who choose to live on their island don't want them. Instead, they live life as simply as possible, with the majority of residents speaking Native Hawaiian as their primary language, or rather, a dialect of Hawaiian specific to Niʻihau. They practice subsistence living, spending the majority of their days fishing or hunting the pigs, cattle, and more exotic oryx and eland that have been brought to the island for big-game hunting.

This preservation of Hawaiian culture takes its toll, however—and it is a very selective preservation. The Robinson family, being descended from missionaries, takes its religious obligations very seriously, and every family living on Niʻihau must attend church every Sunday. Guns, drugs, and alcohol are strictly forbidden, as is growing a beard or wearing your hair long, if you're a man. If you leave Niʻihau for longer than is deemed acceptable by the Robinsons (this can vary), you may not be allowed to return.

And most everyone who lives on Niʻihau wants to continue living there—but they aren't always able to. Money is scarce and jobs are essentially nonexistent. The Robinsons have tried tactic after tactic to create an economy on Niʻihau that won't interfere with life there, but nothing has really worked. The younger generation is leaving, and slowly but surely, the culture is departing with it.

KWAZULU-NATAL

KWAZULU-NATAL, A COASTAL PROVINCE IN SOUTH AFRICA, is one of many places where the ancient practice and profession of traditional African medicine remains prevalent. *Sangomas*, the most commonly used term for traditional practitioners, are proficient in divination, conducting rituals for births and deaths, protecting warriors, counteracting witchcraft, and healing emotional and spiritual, as well as physical, ailments.

There are male and female *sangomas*. They are called to the practice of traditional medicine by contracting an initiation illness, some kind of ailment that resists Western care. If they understand and accept that this illness is a calling, only then will they be healed—and thus begin training. This training period can range from months to several years, during which time the trainee, or *ithwasa*, may not see family, must refrain from sex, and has to undergo intense dedication rituals, including washing in the blood of sacrificed animals and spiritual analysis. At the close of the training period, the *ithwasa* is tested. The *ithwasa*'s family and community are invited to an initiation celebration where a goat is sacrificed to invite the ancestors. The *sangomas* training the *ithwasa* will hide the gallbladder of the sacrificed goat, among other sacred objects, and the *ithwasa* must call upon his or her ancestors to help find them, proving that the *ithwasa* can see beyond the physical world. Only then will the *ithwasa* be accepted as a *sangoma*.

Sangomas receive direction from the ancestors—either the *sangoma*'s personal ancestors or general ancestors of the community—through possession, mediumship, throwing bones, or dream interpretation. A *sangoma* can intercede between the patient and the dead who may be causing the patient's affliction, helping the patient make restitution as needed. Oftentimes, the *sangoma* will then prescribe *muti*, which are botanical or animal remedies. These can include:

GROUND HORSE LEG ◆ to literally kick away bad spirits

LION FAT ◆ for strength, security, and as an antidote to poison

A BLACK CAT ◆ to curse someone

PYTHON SKIN ◆ for protection

But for the most part, *sangomas* keep their remedies secret. Their cures aren't necessarily ingested, but can be added to a bath, used to induce vomiting, inhaled as steam, dried and snorted, applied into small cuts in the skin, or administered via enema.

Sangoma is a Zulu term used colloquially across several cultures, but it specifically means one who practices divination; a healer skilled in herbs is called an *inyanga*, though sometimes the two roles are mixed. Other South African cultures, like Xhosa, Northern and Southern Sotho, Venda, and Tsonga have different names for their *sangomas*, but the roles they play are similar. In all of these cultures, *sangomas* are deeply respected and have a vital position in their communities, for the understanding is that illness of all kinds is caused by witchcraft, contact with impurity, or neglecting one's ancestors—and all can only be healed by a *sangoma*. There are eight times as many traditional healers as Western healers in South Africa, and they are legally recognized. *Sangomas* work in conjunction with Western medicine, helping to combat the spread of HIV/AIDS, diarrhea, and pneumonia.

EARTH CHAKRAS

❖◆❖

THE HUMAN BODY HAS SEVEN CHAKRAS, OR ENERGY CENTERS:
the root chakra, the sacral chakra, the solar plexus chakra, the heart chakra, the throat chakra, the third-eye chakra, and the crown chakra. In fact, every living thing has these seven chakras—including the planet.

If we accept that energy flows through and around everything—for example, gravity, solar energy, magnetic energy, and even tectonic energy—then it follows that there will be energy within the Earth as well. That energy is centered in seven highly charged physical locations around the globe, and just as our human chakras keep us balanced and functioning optimally, so too do the earth chakras maintain the balance and flow of all life.

Ancient civilizations and every indigenous nation on the planet have defined the Earth as a being, sentient and benevolent—a mother. And they have found these epicenters of her energy and erected monuments to her or simply used them as places of worship and spiritual power. We will start, as with the human body, at the base: the root chakra.

MOUNT SHASTA

MOUNT SHASTA IS A NEARLY 15,000-foot-high mountain in Northern California, and it is the root chakra of the world. In humans, the root chakra represents our most instinctive connection to the earth beneath our feet, and Mount Shasta is the base of the Earth's energy system, from which all life stems.

Mount Shasta is within the territories of the Shasta, Wintu, Achumawi, Atsugewi, and Modoc Native American tribes and features heavily in tribal myths and legends, particularly in those of the Wintu, who trace their origins back to a sacred spring on the mountain. Each of the Native American cultures surrounding Mount Shasta tells of its hidden caves and passageways, and the Modoc tell of the Great Spirit Skell, the Spirit of the Above-World, who created Mount Shasta as a stepping-stone from heaven and made his home at its summit. Skell and Llao, the Spirit of the Below-World who lived on Mount Mazama in Oregon, often battled with boulders and lava, leading to the eruption of Mount Mazama resulting in what is now Crater Lake. Despite that lake's beauty, it is thought by the Modoc to be a resting place of evil, while Mount Shasta is a place of light.

Visitors to Mount Shasta claim to have encountered ascended masters and other deeply spiritual beings on the mountain, and it is a center for modern nondenominational worship.

These visitors also see Bigfoot pretty often. Bigfoot can be found all over North America, from Pennsylvania to Florida to Colorado, but it is really only on Mount Shasta that Bigfoot has been seen to levitate, disappear, and pass through solid objects.

But by far the most unusual tale associated with Mount Shasta is the story of Telos, a crystal city that some say is buried within the mountain and inhabited by a race of people called the Lemurians. Supposedly, Lemuria, also called Mu, existed around the same time as the city of Atlantis—reports say that this was anywhere from 400,000 to 8,000 years ago—and was a continent within the Pacific Ocean. According to one story, Lemuria and Atlantis destroyed each other, likely in some kind of thermonuclear war, and their advanced civilizations died with them—almost. The surviving Lemurians hid away in Telos—using those same passageways described in Native American legends.

There are reports of Lemurian sightings around the 1930s; a May 1932 edition of the *L.A. Times* described how the entire side of the mountain lit up, and locals, unsurprised, explained that this was the annual Lemurian Ceremony of Adoration to Gautama—Gautama apparently being America. The locals explained that the seven-foot tall, white-robed, and beautiful Lemurians came to town from time to time to purchase sulphur, salt, and lard from the local stores, paying in gold nuggets. In 1931, a forest fire ravaged much of Mount Shasta, but was stopped in its tracks by a mysterious fog; when the smoke cleared, there was a perfectly visible demarcation zone between the charred and fertile earth. Similarly, saucer-shaped lenticular clouds frequently form above Mount Shasta, and some believe they are either disguised air- or spaceships built by the technologically advanced Lemurians or camouflage for the same.

IN SEARCH OF MAGIC

You can connect with the Earth's chakras by connecting with your own; in doing so, you can bring your own energy into alignment with the planet's, grounding yourself and allowing your energy to rise.

ROOT

If you like, start with aromatherapy. Rub an earthy scent like cedar or clove between your palms and then hold them over your face, breathing deeply. Sit cross-legged on the earth, and breathe deeply, sending your breath, your awareness, and your energy down to your root chakra. Then, get up and do something physical: working in a garden, running, or engaging in whatever form of exercise you prefer.

⇥ SACRAL ⇤

Spread a few drops of sandalwood, sweet orange, or ylang-ylang essential oil at the base of your spine. Find a comfortable position that opens your hips—you could sit with your legs spread wide or with the soles of your feet together—and then straighten your spine as best you can, allowing your hips to unfold, without forcing them. Close your eyes, and send your breath, your awareness, and your energy down to your sacral chakra. And then—dance! You don't have to go full belly dancing—although you can if you want!—just move your body to whatever music inspires it.

⇥ SOLAR PLEXUS ⇤

Ginger, lemon, and chamomile are excellent for the solar plexus. You can use essential oils or drink tea—whatever you feel best serves you. For your moment of meditation, find a position that you can hold comfortably while still engaging your core; this can be anything from a forearm plank to simply sitting or standing with attention on firming up your solar plexus. Allow yourself to breathe, and send that breath, that awareness, that energy to you solar plexus chakra. For a bit extra, do some crunches, some bicycles, or any other core exercise you enjoy!

⇥ HEART ⇤

Rose and bergamot are both excellent scents to engage your heart chakra. Rub a little essential oil on your palms and bring your hands over your heart. Take deep breaths, filling your chest. This is your central chakra, and all springs from here. Send your breath, your awareness, and your energy to your heart. And then get that heart pumping! Get some fresh blood moving through your body by going for a run, a bike ride, or a swim.

⇥ THROAT ⇤

Rub a little lavender, clary sage, or neroli essential oil in the hollow at the base of your throat. Gently roll your neck, moving your head in a circle. Bring your chin to your chest, and then open your throat to the sky. Which feels best? Choose, and then send your breath, your awareness, and your energy there: closed and protected or open and exposed— whichever feels right for you at this moment. If you like, sing! You can sing to yourself privately, or get a group of friends together for some karaoke.

⇥ THIRD EYE ⇤

Your third eye is located in front of your pineal gland, at the space right above the center of your brow. Jasmine, vetiver, and rosemary are excellent scents for opening your third eye. Rub a drop of essential oil on each of your index fingers. Starting at your third eye, draw lines across your brow over to your temples. Close your two eyes to open your third. Send your breath, your awareness, and your energy to that place that connects you with your creativity. And then, spend some time in silence exploring that creativity, either with a new craft project or a new line of study.

⇥ CROWN ⇤

Frankincense and myrrh are powerful scents that can help us connect with the world beyond what is immediately present and obvious. Rub a little on the soles of your feet, for though this is the part of your body farthest from your crown, it is where your pores are largest and most receptive. If you can lie flat for a time without falling asleep, do so, otherwise stand with the top of your head reaching for the sky. Send your breath, your awareness, and your energy up from the soles of your feet, passing each chakra on the way through your body, up to the crown of your head, and then past it, to the unseen world beyond. Meditate like this for as long as you like.

LAKE TITICACA

LAKE TITICACA IS AN ENORMOUS, VERY DEEP LAKE ON THE border of Bolivia and Peru, and it is the sacral chakra of the planet. The human sacral chakra acts as the center of our fertility and creativity, and for the Earth, it is much the same; this is the energetic origin of new species and of evolutional shifts in species. Lake Titicaca was the birthing place of South American ancient civilizations like the Inca, and remnants of temples can be found on its shores— and even in its depths.

An Incan creation myth describes the god Con Tiqui Viracocha emerging from Lake Titicaca, bringing humans with him. After commanding the sun, moon, and stars to rise, Viracocha created more human beings from stone, commanding them to go forth and populate the world. Their spirits would return to the lake at the end of their lives. The Isla del Sol in the center of the lake (and hence, the center of the sacral chakra) is the home of Inti, the Incan sun god, and the island is essentially a labyrinth of stones and temples, having been used as a place of worship by Incan priests. The south side of the island is home to the Inca Steps, a stone staircase 206 steps long, leading up to a sacred fountain. And on the Isla de la Luna, home of the moon goddess Mama Killa, is the House of the Chosen Virgins of the Sun, where women would go to live a secluded, nunlike existence.

The lake's underwater temple, however, dates back to between 1,000 and 1,500 years ago, predating the Inca. The Tiwanaku people would have built this, and their temple is about the size of two soccer fields. As long ago as that was, it would certainly have been *after* the lake came into existence. It is believed that there is also a giant golden disc beneath the lake, holding the capacity to create powerful earthquakes, even perhaps shifting the rotation of the planet, as it could receive information directly from Con Tiqui Viracocha. The disc contains the DNA of the world.

ULURU

ALSO KNOWN AS AYERS ROCK, ULURU, A MASSIVE SANDSTONE monolith in Australia, is the world's solar plexus chakra. For humans, the third chakra is our source of confidence, personal power, and choice; thus, Uluru is deeply powerful. Nearby Kata Tjuta, a group of smaller but still enormous sandstone monoliths, is also tied in with this chakra.

Uluru is a living cultural landscape sacred to the Anangu people, also known as the Pitjantjatjara people, some of the most ancient indigenous people on Earth with a culture dating back 60,000 years. According to their traditions, Uluru was formed by ancestral beings during the Dreamtime, or when the Earth was first coming into being. The bodies of their ancestors are woven into the rock, and according to Aboriginal beliefs, all life as it is today can be traced back to these ancestors of the Dreamtime. The Dreamtime was—and is, as Aboriginal people dream—the beginning of knowledge, from which came the laws of existence.

These ancestors created man and beast as they formed Uluru, and they are represented by totemic creatures. Most of the southern face of Uluru was created by the battle between the Liru (poisonous snakes) and the Kunia (carpet snakes), while the Linga (sand lizard) and the Metalungana (sleeping lizard) formed smaller parts of the southern face. Most of the mountain's northern face was created by the Mala (hare-wallaby) people, Tjinderi-tjinderiba (willy-wagtail woman), and her children, as well as Kulpunya (dingo), who destroyed most of the Mala, and Lunba (kingfisher woman), who tried to protect them. The formation of the western face is associated with Kandju (another sand lizard), while Itjari-tjari (mole) created a number of caves and potholes on the surface of the western side. The camps of the first male and female couple, the Kaldidi, were transformed into a boulder pile on the southwestern corner.

The Kunia people have Dreamtime stories about every single rock and crack on Uluru. Boulders in Tjukiki Gorge were ancient Kunia women, and their wooden calabash is a tall slab of rock at the head of the gorge. Their pubic hairs became the low bushes on the floor of the gorge, and their campfire became Kapi Tjukiki, the Rockhole.

A long boulder on the plain around Uluru was a Kunia woman, and a smaller boulder, her children. An old Kunia woman and old Kunia man lying asleep in the sun became another long boulder. The deep ridges on the sides of Uluru were once the tracks made by the carpet-snake people as they traveled to and from the Uluru Waterhole. The gutters on the sides of the rock are the beards of old men. There is a large split boulder on the southeast side of Uluru, and it is said that a Kunia woman named Minma Bulari gave birth to a child there. The cave within the split boulder was Bulari's womb, and its opening her vagina—there are light markings along the opening that are the knee indentations of her midwife. The infant is the irregularly shaped rock near the mouth of the cave, and Bulari's carrying dish is a hollowed boulder nearby. Pregnant women now try to give birth in the cave in the belief that Bulari will protect them and provide an easy and safe delivery.

It is legal in Australia to climb Uluru, but against the wishes of the Anangu people. They have left a giant sign—which thousands of people walk right past every day—saying: "We, the traditional Anangu owners, have this to say. Uluru is sacred in our culture, a place of great knowledge. Under our traditional law, climbing is not permitted. This is our home. Please don't climb."

STONEHENGE

THE MOST RECOGNIZABLY MAGICAL PLACE IN THE WESTERN world, Stonehenge in Salisbury, England, serves as the heart chakra of the planet, though the surrounding areas of Dorset, Glastonbury, and Shaftesbury are part of the widespread heart chakra; Glastonbury is or was said to be the home of the Holy Grail, and there are dozens of other ancient places of power and worship in the vicinity. This central chakra balances the other six, as it connects the first three earthy chakras with the more heavenly final three. In humans, this is the love chakra, and in the Earth, that love is expressed as powerful energy. Why else would these enormous, twenty-five-ton rocks be brought 150 miles from what is now Wales to this precise spot?

Stonehenge consists of eighty stones, arranged as one open circle containing another that falls within it, like two C-shapes facing each other. Archaeologists have determined that the site was used for a burial ground before the

stones were brought here some 2,500 years ago and there was likely a wooden version of the henge as early as 8,500 years ago; at some point it might have been fifteen times the size it is today. Obviously, there are no written records of how Stonehenge functioned back then, but we can make some deductions: The site is aligned to the sunset of the winter solstice and the sunrise of the summer solstice, and the pagan holidays of Yule and Litha are celebrated on those days, respectively. The Heel Stone, also known as the Sun Stone, at the northeast section of the outer circle, is rougher than most of the others, about sixteen feet high, and leans toward the inner circle. At the summer solstice, someone standing within the circle would see the sun rising above this precise stone. Scholars and archaeologists studying Stonehenge agree on very little, but they all concur that it was certainly used to mark and predict celestial events.

It has also been suggested that Stonehenge was a place of healing and/or preparation for death. The bluestones brought from Wales originate from a place called Maenclochog, which translates to "ringing rock"—and the rocks of Stonehenge do indeed ring. When struck, they respond with a loud clanging noise; lithophones like this were often considered healing stones, and giant ones would have been unimaginably powerful. Some bodies buried beneath Stonehenge come from as far away as the Mediterranean Sea, Germany, and Brittany and show signs of illness or damage, making it likely that folk would travel great distances to Stonehenge in times of suffering. Geoffrey of Monmouth, a British cleric and historian who lived around AD 1100, postulated that this journey to Stonehenge was part of a ritual, a passage from life to death, celebrating with past ancestors and those who had passed more recently.

Today, thousands of people gather at Stonehenge for both summer and winter solstices, to worship, heal, and connect with the power of the Earth and the power of the past.

THE GREAT PYRAMID

THE GREAT PYRAMID OF GIZA AND THE NEARBY SPHINX, AS well as Mount Sinai in Egypt and the Mount of Olives in Jerusalem, all vibrate with the energy of the Earth's throat chakra. In humans this chakra is the center of our voice, of our power to communicate. How does the Earth communicate? There are many places of unrest in the world, but the Middle East is inarguably one of the most challenging, as multiple cultures, nations, and religions fight for ownership of this fifth chakra. It would seem that if the Earth is speaking to us, we are having a hard time hearing her over our own voices.

For more than 3,800 years, the Great Pyramid was the tallest man-made structure on Earth. It was built over a period of ten to twenty years, around 2500 BC, and served as a tomb for the pharaoh Khufu. The sides of the square base are aligned to the four cardinal directions, and like Stonehenge, its perfect construction despite the primitive tools available to its builders confounds historians. The Sphinx, on the other hand, was cut from bedrock, likely also around 2500 BC for the pharaoh Khafra, the son of Khufu. Of course, it wasn't called the Sphinx at the time; it was referred to as a *shesep-ankh*, or living image—perhaps the face carved into the rock was Khafra, or perhaps it was someone else. A thousand years later, it was honored as a symbol of the sun god Horus. But the Sphinx is almost impossible to date accurately because, unlikely as it may seem for such an impressive monument, there are almost no ancient accounts of its existence. The famous historian Herodotus makes no mention of it, and neither do any other Greek historians.

Mount Sinai was the place where God spoke to Moses from a burning bush; it was also where Moses received the Ten Commandments, as well as instructions for how he should build the Ark of the Covenant to contain them. This is, perhaps, the throat chakra of the Earth at its most understandable, while the Mount of Olives in Jerusalem echoes with dispute. Mount Olivet had been sacred

to the ancient kingdom of Judah and was used as a burial ground for Jews for thousands of years. It also was the site of many significant events in Jesus's life, including his ascension. It is thought that the Resurrection will begin there. Similarly, in Muslim tradition, it is believed that a bridge with seven arches will span from the Mount of Olives to the Temple Mount in Jerusalem. This bridge will be no wider than a single hair, and the righteous will cross over it to heaven.

GLASTONBURY TOR

THE THIRD-EYE CHAKRA OF THE PLANET IS UNUSUAL—IT TENDS to move. The Earth shifts slightly with each solstice and equinox, and the culmination of these shifts is the beginning of a new aeon or age, a period of time when the sun is aligned with a certain constellation of the zodiac; we are now, as the song says, in the Age of Aquarius, which began in 1447 AD and will end in 3597 AD. During this age, the third-eye chakra is in Glastonbury, England, hovering near the heart chakra.

For humans, the third-eye chakra represents our ability to see things clearly, with wisdom. As such, the mobile third-eye chakra of the Earth is our planet's way of deeply observing the workings on her surface. Glastonbury Tor is a conical hill topped by a fourteenth-century church tower. Until two thousand years ago, the Tor was surrounded by an ocean, which eventually dwindled to a lake and then became the flat field that it is today. The Tor is constructed of seven levels of terraces encircling the hill, dating back to the Neolithic period. They appear to follow a sort of diagram, much like Stonehenge. An old Celtic name for Glastonbury is Ynys-witrin, "the isle of glass." Gwyn ap Nudd, ruler of the underworld, was said to dwell there. He was the leader of the Wild Hunt, which flew across the night sky gathering souls to take back to the Tor, where they would then pass on. Legends correlate Gwyn ap Nudd with the King of the Fairies, who lived under the hill of the Tor. The hollow under the hill was called Annwn, or Avalon. Today, visitors to the Tor still search for the entrance to Annwn.

Avalon, of course, also features heavily in King Arthur legends. It was here that Joseph of Arimathea came from Jerusalem, bearing the Holy Grail. He slept at the base of the Tor, having thrust his staff into the ground; by morning, it had sprouted into a strange thornbush, now known as the Glastonbury Thorn— an odd hawthorn tree that blooms not once, but twice per year. Joseph buried the Grail at the base of the Tor, the entrance to the Underworld, and the Grail poured forth from the earth a spring, now known as the Chalice Well or the Red Spring—a red-tinted source of healing.

The tower atop the Tor is quite phallic, while the well is feminine, and so the Tor is often worshipped today as a place where the Divine Masculine and the Divine Feminine come together. Visitors often see dancing balls of light, luminous, active, and even sentient. Perhaps they are fairy lights.

MOUNT KAILASH

THE FINAL AND MOST POWERFUL SITE IS MOUNT KAILASH IN
Tibet, the crown chakra of the Earth. Our crown chakra is our human connection
with the world of spirit, magic, and power. It is the Earth's connection with this
power and also with us; it is here that our link is made manifest—in the form of
a sharp peak in the tallest mountain range in the world. Mount Kailash is the
axis mundi, literally the axis of the world, providing an intersection between the
physical and the spiritual.

Mount Kailash is sacred to a variety of religions; it is the home of the Hindu
god Shiva, the Tantric meditational being Demchog, and the Bön sky goddess
Sipaimen. It is the navel of the world for Buddhists and the first place of enlightenment for Jains. Its four flat, black faces mark the four cardinal directions.
Rising over 22,000 feet, Mount Kailash is probably the most sacred place on
the planet . . . and it is the least visited. It is forbidden to climb the mountain,
though a few thousand reach its base every year. There, they walk around the
mountain, in a ritual called a Kora or Parikrama. This thirty-two-mile trek can
be done in three days, walking clockwise for Hindus and Buddhists, and coun-
terclockwise for Bönpos and Jains. For some, the circumnavigation takes three
weeks, as the pilgrim begins by kneeling, lying prostrate, and making a mark in
the earth. He or she then rises back to kneeling, prays, crawls forward to the
mark in the earth, only to begin the process again. And for practitioners of
a sacred and secret breathing practice called Lung-gom, the journey can be
made in just one day. It is said that anyone who can complete 108 Koras will
reach enlightenment.

At the base of the mountain are two lakes: Lake Manasarovar is freshwater
and perfectly round. Lake Rakshastal is salt water and shaped like a crescent
moon. Together, the lakes represent the light and the darkness. Manasarovar is
said to be always serene, while Rakshastal froths and rages.

LEY LINES

◆●◆

LEY LINES ARE, ESSENTIALLY, MYSTICAL LATITUDE AND LONGITUDE *and they tend to follow the path of the sun. The most powerful mystical places on Earth fall on these lines, and with the exception of the third-eye chakra, all the Earth's chakras sit on a place where at least two lines intersect.*

There are hundreds, perhaps even thousands of ley lines. While these lines appear straight, they actually curve around the world, with two major ley lines acting as arteries for the others. The Rainbow Serpent Line, which is charged with feminine energy, arcs from the South Pacific, up through South America and across to England, and back down through Tibet and Australia. The Plumed Serpent Line moves in the opposite direction, from the Northern Pacific, down through Mount Shasta, crossing through the Rainbow Serpent Line at Lake Titicaca, and moving up through South Africa, Bali, and Japan. These two lines are powered by five Gates—places of high energy that feed them.

Most cultures throughout the world reference these lines in one way or another. They are known as fairy roads and corpse roads in Western Europe, turingas or songlines in Australia, Dragon Lines in China, Spirit Lines in Peru, and heilige linien in Germany. Nightmarchers, or huaka'i pō, walk them in Hawai'i. The Inca had ceques, and the Maya had sacbe. Along each ley line, and frequently at the intersections of two or more, are locales that vibrate with energy. They are often holy sites, dating back thousands of years—but their power can still be felt today.

WISTMAN'S WOOD

WISTMAN'S WOOD IN DEVON, ENGLAND, FALLS
along the St. Michael's Alignment, part of what is now frequently called the Rainbow Serpent Line. This gorgeous, moss-covered ancient forest with gnarled trees and treacherous footing is the source of dozens of tales of the supernatural. Visitors have seen processions of robed, monk-like figures walking the corpse road to nearby Lydford.

It is said that locals know not to venture near the "Wood of the Wisemen" after dark, for it is the place from which hellhounds venture forth. Stories of these hounds inspired Sir Arthur Conan Doyle's *Hound of the Baskervilles*; the Wisht Hounds hunt the moors in search of lost souls, much like the Wild Hunt of the fairies. These huge, black, red-eyed dogs can be heard at night, baying for blood. Children can be protected from their attacks by keeping a crust of bread beneath their pillow.

Wistman's Wood is treacherous to walk through, which is partly why it has remained untouched for so many years. Uneven, moss-covered boulders give way to deep cracks, which are said to be swarming with poisonous adders. But legends say that the wood was at one point a meeting place for ancient Druids to gather and worship. In a place filled with boulders, the largest is known as the Druid's Stone or the Buller Stone; it is there that they supposedly conducted their most mysterious rituals.

KUKANILOKO

IN THE MIDDLE OF AN ABANDONED SUGARCANE FIELD ON THE Hawaiian island of Oʻahu, you'll find a small field of relatively normal-looking rocks. But these rocks are sacred, for it is said that a child born in this place would be full of mana, or spiritual power, and would be a strong and good leader.

The birthing stones in Kukaniloko were a place of delivery for Hawaiian chieftesses, beginning in the twelfth century and continuing up until the seventeenth. There are two rows of eighteen rocks and a massive center rock. An *aliʻi* woman about to give birth would lie against the largest stone, padded for support and surrounded by attendants. The birth would be witnessed by the thirty-six chiefs of Oʻahu, as they watched from the other thirty-six stones. Kukaniloko translates to "anchor the cry from within," and the mother would give birth in silence, keeping her cry anchored.

Kukaniloko is at the center of the island, and as such provides a wide view of the surrounding mountains, valleys, and skies. Astronomers from the University of Hawaiʻi studied several markings found on the stones and determined that the site was likely also used as a kind of Stonehenge, tracking the movements of the stars to mark the Hawaiian calendar.

The island chain of Hawaiʻi lies directly on a smaller ley line referred to as the 19.47 degree ley line. This line cuts across the center of the two major ley lines, aligning with the pyramid at Teotihuacán, Mexico, among other sacred sites.

HALEAKALĀ

HALEAKALĀ, WHICH TRANSLATES TO "THE HOUSE OF THE SUN," is a massive, dormant shield volcano forming much of the island of Maui in Hawai'i. Like Kukaniloko, it lies on the 19.47 degree ley line, but it also functions as a Gate, a place of energy that powers the two main ley lines.

Ancient Hawaiian culture is filled with creation myths, and many of them involve Maui, the "Hawaiian Superman." According to one legend, Lā, the sun, liked to rush through his journey; he would sleep in, hurry across the sky, and go back to bed. Maui's mother, Hina, couldn't get all her work done in such short days, and neither could the Hawaiian people. So Maui climbed up Haleakalā and lay in wait. As Lā began his first ascent, Maui lassoed him, tying him to the ground. They came to an agreement: for half the year, Lā would take his time, moving slowly across the sky, and for the other half of the year, he could move a little faster, getting home to his rest.

The most powerful experience Haleakalā has to offer is available to anyone willing to make the journey. Depending on the speed at which Lā is traveling, arrive early enough so that it is still dark and the stars are out. Watch as the stars slowly vanish in the changing shades of the gradually brightening sky, until the first rays of the sun appear over the horizon.

BALI

BALI LIES AT THE INTERSECTION OF THE TWO MAJOR LEY LINES, both the Plumed Serpent and the Rainbow Serpent, and like Haleakalā, it functions as a Gate, powering those lines. A relatively small island in Indonesia, Bali is one of the most spiritual places on Earth; there are at least 11,000 temples on the island. The indigenous people of Bali, along with the Austronesians who colonized the island around 5,000 years ago, have absorbed Mahayana Buddhism, Shaivism, Tantrism, and Hinduism. The Balinese religion is an amalgam of all of these, along with the island's ancient indigenous practices.

The tallest of the four mountains on Bali is Mount Agung, home of Batara Gunung Agung, also called Mahadewa, the supreme manifestation of Shiva. The people of Bali believe Mount Agung is a replica of Mount Meru, the axis of the physical, metaphysical, and spiritual universes sacred to the Buddhist, Hindu, and Jain religions. The temple complex of Pura Besakih rests on Mount Agung's slopes; parts of Pura Besakih are at least 2,000 years old, dating back to before Hindus arrived in Bali. Mount Agung is an active volcano; in 1963, its eruptions killed 1,700 people, but the temple remained miraculously untouched. There is a triple shrine, called a *meru* (named for Mount Meru) within the courtyard of one of the temples in Pura Besakih. This elaborate shrine is dedicated to Shiva, and it consists of several tiers, each constructed in a different type of wood appropriate to its function, with ceremonies around each tier.

Mount Batur, also an active volcano, is a holy place for the indigenous people living in the remote jungles of nearby Lake Batur. Both locations are sacred to Dewi Danu, the Goddess of the Lake. She, along with her natural springs, feeds the rivers that provide most of Bali's water. Tirta Empul, a Hindu temple here dedicated to Vishnu, contains a *petirtaan* in which visitors can bathe in its holy springwater for ritual purification and healing.

PALENQUE

THE ANCIENT RUINS OF PALENQUE FORM A GATE ON THE PLUMED
Serpent ley line. Lakamha, as it was once known, was a Maya city-state in the seventh century, though the ruins here date back to as early as 250 BC. Although there are larger ruins in parts of South America, this Mexican site is in the best shape and contains some of the most intricate carvings and architecture. This ancient, elegant city has a planned urban layout, including residential, funerary, medical, and ritual areas. The buildings have vaulted roofs, stucco scenes on friezes, columns, and walls, T-shaped windows, and other rich decoration.

Maya culture is renowned today for its mathematical ingenuity and complex astronomical understanding, including the calendar. Many of the temples and other structures of Palenque are aligned with certain constellations. At the center of Palenque is a series of structures known as the Palace; the aristocracy likely used this complex of several connected buildings for governing, entertainment, and religious ceremonies. The tallest structure in Palenque, in the center of the Palace, is thought to have been an astronomical observatory. Rising four stories high, an observer standing in this tower on the day of the winter solstice would see the sun set directly over the giant tiered pyramid known as the Temple of Inscriptions. Like the Egyptian pyramids, the Temple of Inscriptions was a tomb, in this case for K'inich Janaab' Pakal, seventh-century ruler of Palenque. Pakal, who ruled for an astonishing seventy years, was buried with a jade mask beneath a sarcophagus depicting himself lying atop an "earth monster," with the open jaws of a jaguar, the totem of Xibalba, the Underworld. The World Tree found in so many early cultures stands above him, and in it is perched Vucub-Caquix, a bird that represents the space between light and darkness—which is the space Pakal inhabits at the moment of his death.

Archaeologists have uncovered and restored only a very small portion of the city of Palenque—who knows what else they may find?

SEDONA

THE RED ROCKS OF SEDONA, ARIZONA, ARE SAID TO CONTAIN
up to fifteen vortices, or places where multiple ley lines intersect, most prominently the Plumed Serpent ley line. The most powerful vortices are Airport Mesa, Cathedral Rock, Boynton Canyon, and Bell Rock. The outcroppings were given these names in 1980 by a local medium named Page Bryant—but their power was acknowledged long before that time, as the Navajo, Yavapai, and Hopi tribes considered these sites places of power, holding sacred ceremonies there.

Airport Mesa is the most accessible to visitors, given that it's close to the center of Sedona proper. The mesa is filled with twisted juniper trees that swirl with the energy from the vortex. Some visitors see colored orbs, but in general the energy at Airport Mesa is one of upflow, helping you find a higher perspective, as well as a sense of serenity. It's a masculine energy, allowing you to become more decisive, empowered, and active.

Cathedral Rock, also called Red Rock Crossing, is more difficult to access, given that it's a pretty steep climb. You don't have to get to the very top, or the saddle, to feel the vortex, but the energy is most powerful there. Cathedral Rock has a softer, more feminine energy and will enhance both your intuition and your compassion.

Boynton Canyon, particularly the space between the thirty-foot-high knoll just past its entrance and a formation called Kachina Woman, contains a balance of these energies. The space between the masculine and feminine, between yin and yang, allows for a stronger whole, in the same way that the opposing forces of an archway can support a greater weight.

Bell Rock, a distinctive towering formation, is also covered with junipers, but the energy here is in greater balance: the masculine, the feminine, and the space in between are all very powerful in this place. Although you can climb Bell Rock and there are several hiking trails, it isn't necessary to go all the way up to the top to experience the vortex. Visitors frequently report UFOs, odd glowing green clouds, as well as powerful feelings of joy and ecstasy.

ANGKOR WAT

THE TEMPLE COMPLEX OF ANGKOR WAT in Cambodia is the largest religious monument in the world, and it is located along the Rainbow Serpent ley line. It was originally constructed in the early twelfth century as a Hindu temple dedicated to Vishnu, but by the end of the century it was being used for Buddhist spiritual practices. Legend has it that this city of temples was constructed in a single night by a divine architect, and that it was designed to resemble Mount Meru.

It appears that the placement of the main temples of Angkor Wat mirror the stars of the constellation Draco as it would have appeared in the sky at the spring equinox of 10,500 BC. Now this is obviously long before Angkor Wat was built, but as we've seen with Stonehenge and many other sites, temples are often built atop previous temples, again and again.

And indeed, archaeologists have recently discovered the remains of ancient cities beneath the rain forest floor not far from Angkor Wat. This discovery constitutes a new understanding of a planned urban landscape connecting these temple cities. Moss-covered remains of elephant statues, canals, gardens, and roads reveal an entirely new understanding of a civilization that was essentially a mystery.

MOUNT FUJI

THE BEAUTIFUL MOUNT FUJI IN JAPAN FALLS ALONG THE PLUMED
Serpent ley line, where it functions as a Gate. Its unusually symmetrical cone rises above an active volcano. The origin of the name "Fuji" is something of a mystery, as the moniker predates the kanji currently in use and could be defined as many things—anything from "immortal" to "unequaled." One theory is that the name comes from the Ainu people, a Japanese indigenous group, and refers to their goddess of fire. It is perhaps out of respect for this goddess that women were not permitted to climb Mount Fuji until the late nineteenth century.

The mountain hosts a number of deities, including the goddess Sakuya-hime, daughter of the mountain god Ohoyamatsumi and the goddess of the cherry blossom. Legend has it that Sakuya-hime met and enchanted Ninigi, the grandson of the sun goddess, but her father refused the match, suggesting instead Sakuya-hime's sister Iwa-naga-hime, goddess of stone. But Ninigi had his heart set, and so he and Sakuya-hime were married. (Incidentally, his choice of the more delicate goddess is why humans are said to live such short, fragile lives). Sakuya-hime bore three children. The emperors of Japan, who still preside over the country today, trace their line directly back to her.

Not all of Mount Fuji's energy is positive, however. At the northwest foot of the mountain lies Aokigahara, known as the "Suicide Forest." Since the 1950s, more than 500 people have died in the forest, mostly by their own hands, and the Japanese government has taken to putting up signs encouraging visitors to the "Sea of Trees" to seek help. In the nineteenth century, families who could not support their elders abandoned them there, a tragic practice called *ubasute*. Infanticide may also have occurred. Local police search the forest for bodies, to ease the spirits of the dead and comfort their remaining family members, but it is believed that many bodies are never found.

But if the bodies are not recovered, and if someone dies in a state of anger or sadness, then they are said to become *yurei*, ghosts who wander forever, unable to be appeased. There are those who believe that Aokigahara is so filled with *yurei* that they have saturated the trees themselves.

→⊱ IN SEARCH OF MAGIC ⊰←

If ley lines are everywhere, how do we find them? There are a couple of different methods. Alfred Watkins, who coined the term, started by mapping out all the different magical, holy, haunted, or otherwise high-energy places in his area. Get out a local map, and mark those locations that fit the bill. You might find that they hover around a central point, and that point is a vortex of some kind, or you might find that they fall in a fairly straight line.

You can also try dowsing. Dowsing is an ancient way of finding groundwater, minerals, or ores hidden beneath the ground, and it is an effective way of tracking energy. Start by finding or creating a dowsing rod. If you have a small Y-shaped branch, that will work, but it is best if the branch is from the area in which you will be dowsing and generally should not be cut from a living tree. If this isn't available, you can use a metal hanger to create two L-shaped rods.

If you're using the branch, hold it loosely with one fork of the Y in each hand. If you're using the rods, hold the shorter length of the L loosely in each hand. Take a deep breath, clearing your own energy so that you don't influence the rods. Hold your arms up parallel to your shoulders, but keep them relaxed. If you're using the metal rods, hold your hands about shoulder-width apart. The metal rods will cross toward each other when you pass a point of energy, while the branch will arc upward. Follow those points, document them as you go, and you will track your line.

LAKE TAUPO

LAKE TAUPO FILLS THE CALDERA OF MOUNT TAUPO, A DORMANT
volcano on the North Island of New Zealand. It is a Gate on the Rainbow Serpent
Line. The lake is a *taonga*, a treasured site honored by the Ngati Tuwharetoa tribe,
descendants of the navigator Ngatoroirangi who led his people to Aotearoa
(New Zealand) from Hawaiki (not to be confused with Hawai'i, this instead refers
to Raiatea, near Tahiti).

It is said that Ngatoroirangi created Lake Taupo. Upon his arrival in
Aotearoa, he looked for a suitable place to live, but there was nothing on the
mountain but a dust bowl. He hurled a totara tree into the caldera, where its
branches pierced the earth, releasing a stream of water filling Taupo *moana*,
the Sea of Taupo, and then pulled loose strands from his cloak and tossed them
into the lake, where they swam away as fish. His people now had an abundant
supply of food and water.

Today, Lake Taupo is still owned by the
Ngati Tuwharetoa. In the late 1970s, Matahi
Whakataka-Brightwell and John Randall
carved a ten-meter-high likeness of
Ngatoroirangi into the cliff face over
the lake, so that he could continue to
protect his people.

TABLE MOUNTAIN

TABLE MOUNTAIN IN CAPE TOWN AT THE TIP OF SOUTH AFRICA is at the southernmost dip of the Plumed Serpent Line and functions as the ley line's final Gate. It is an eerily flat plateau rising over the city that is flanked by two peaks: Devil's Peak to the east and Lion's Head to the west.

The Xhosa, a South African ethnic group, tell of the god Qamata, the creator of the world. As he was working away, a sea dragon called Nkanyamba, who wanted the planet to remain covered in water, interrupted him. They fought, but Nkanyamba was too strong for Qamata. Jobela, Qamata's mother, created four giants to protect the earth Qamata had created, and Nkanyamba gave up and retreated. Those giants then turned to stone, standing as sentinels against Nkanyamba's return. Umlindi Wemingizimu, the Watcher of the South, still stands as Table Mountain.

Another story, thought to have originated from the Cape Malay ethnic group, is far more whimsical. The flat top of Table Mountain often collects clouds above, acting as a sort of tablecloth, and the story goes that a retired Dutch pirate named Van Hunks spent many a day smoking on the slopes of Devil's Peak. He was challenged to a smoking duel by a stranger, and the two of them spent days filling and refilling their pipes and smoking them, so much so that they created a cloud of smoke that enveloped the entire mountain. Van Hunks won, but as is often the case with contests with a stranger, that stranger turned out to be the Devil, and he was not pleased to have been beaten. Instead of granting a skill like guitar-playing, he brought down a bolt of lightning, taking Van Hunks with him back to Hell.

CONCLUSION

For as long as we have walked the Earth, we have believed it to be magical. We have told countless legends and found the most amazing places, both natural and man-made, some of them almost too beautiful to be real. And to this day, there are still things we cannot explain, phenomena that aren't *quite* accounted for by science and yet clearly exist.

We should never discount our own senses. When we feel something is *wrong*, that there is an odd and awful feeling about a place, we often learn later that something terrible happened there. A sunny spot in the bustling French Quarter of New Orleans can give you a chill . . . because it was the site of a slave auction. A forest in Japan that is as beautiful and peaceful as any other can call dozens of people to die in its shadows every year. An empty field with a few rocks in Hawai'i can echo with the stifled screams of powerful women, and a devil can be spotted in the swampy forests of New Jersey.

But more often than not, we feel awe instead of fear. We are healed by the waters of Lourdes and the Ganges River, and we find peace and inspiration in Sedona and Stonehenge. Whether ley lines or earth chakras are the cause, whether gods have granted power to certain places, or whether Lemurians from deep within Mount Shasta are behind it all, there is magic in the sacred places of the earth. We tell stories about these places, and we are drawn to them for thousands upon thousands of years, because there is *something* happening there.

Whether you decide to visit some of these places or not, seek out the ones around you in everyday life. The forest behind your house, the river flowing through your city, or even just the street corner on your way to the store may spark something in you or resonate with an energy, a power, a *magic*. Lean into it, explore it, and see what it brings you.

ACKNOWLEDGMENTS

To the lovely Shannon Connors Fabricant, thank you for accompanying me on this journey—each book with you is more magical than the last! To Kristin Kiser for her everlasting support, Susan Van Horn for her impeccable design work, Ashley Benning for being a hawk-eyed double-checker extraordinaire, Amy Cianfrone for getting the magic out into the world, and everyone else at Running Press for being, well, the best.

Katie Vernon, I'm a huge fan. Thank you so much for making this book so stunning.

Thank you to Kelly Notaras, Rachel Mehl, and Chandika Devi for boosting me up.

Thank you Dave and Maile for coming with me on my armchair travels, and some actual ones, too. Thank you Dad for all those times you *didn't* make fun of me. I'm sure they existed, even if I didn't know about them. Thank you to my sister, Hannah, for turning off your phone while LeBron was playing. I know it's hard. And most of all, thank you to my mom, for being willing to go to all those graveyards and voodoo shops with me. It's not devilry, I promise.

PHOTO CREDITS

FAIRYTALE LOCALES
Hinatuan Enchanted River: page 5, raksybH/iStock/Getty Images Plus
Fairy Glen: pages 6–7, MarcelloLand/iStock/Getty Images Plus
Giant's Causeway: pages 10–11, elementals/iStock/Getty Images Plus
Plain of Jars: pages 12–13, vidalidali/iStock/Getty Images Plus
Swat River: pages 16–17, SAKhanPhotography/iStock/Getty Images Plus
Pennard Castle: page 18, leighcol/iStock/Getty Images Plus
Yeun Elez: pages 22–23, Gwengoat/iStock/Getty Images Plus
Ha Long Bay: page 25, ryasnik/iStock/Getty Images Plus
Llyn y Fan Fach: pages 26–27, leighcol/iStock/Getty Images Plus

PLACES OF HEALING
Chimayó: page 32, Michael Warren/iStock/Getty Images Plus
Ganges River: page 36, Neosiam/iStock/Getty Images Plus
Killin: page 41, alanfin/iStock/Getty Images Plus

MAGIC IN NATURE
Hang Son Doong: pages 44–45, Geng Xu/iStock/Getty Images Plus
Pink Lakes: page 46, KonArt/iStock/Getty Images Plus
Sea of Stars: page 49, tdub_video/E+/Getty Images
Tianzi Mountain: pages 50–51, Top Photo Corporation/Top Photo Group/Getty Images Plus
Salar de Uyuni: page 53, Onfokus/E+/Getty Images
Gorëme: pages 54–55, dem10/E+/Getty Images
Waitomo: pages 58–59, MarcelStrelow/iStock/Getty Images Plus
The Door to Hell: pages 60–61, Iwanami_Photos/iStock/Getty Images Plus

HAUNTED PLACES
Paris catacombs: page 66, Dirk94025/iStock/Getty Images Plus
Davelis Cave: pages 70–71, Electrofear/iStock/Getty Images Plus
Cannock Chase: pages 74–75, iharvo/iStock/Getty Images Plus
Bhangar Ruins: page 78, ThomasFluegge/iStock/Getty Images Plus
Pine Barrens: page 83, Stanley45/iStock/Getty Images Plus

THE PAST IN THE PRESENT
Graz: page 91, bririemoments/iStock/Getty Images Plus
Madagascar: pages 94–95, Óscar Royuela/iStock/Getty Images Plus
Mexico City: pages 98–99, BeteMarques/iStock/Getty Images Plus

EARTH CHAKRAS
Mount Shasta: pages 106–107, Joecho-16/iStock/Getty Images Plus
Lake Titicaca: page 112, Zaharov/iStock/Getty Images Plus
Uluru: page 115, simonbradfield/iStock Unreleased
Stonehenge: page 118, davidevison/iStock/Getty Images Plus
The Great Pyramid: page 121, PeskyMonkey/E+/Getty Images
Glastonbury Tor: page 123, Blackbeck/iStock/Getty Images Plus
Mount Kailash: page 124, Lihana/iStock/Getty Images Plus

LEY LINES
Wistman's Wood: pages 128–129, Stanley45/iStock/Getty Images Plus
Bali: page 133, Michel de Ridder/iStock/Getty Images Plus
Palenque: page 134, SerafinoMozzo/iStock/Getty Images Plus
Sedona: page 137, wingedwolf/iStock/Getty Images Plus
Angkor Wat: pages 138–139, boule13/iStock/Getty Images Plus
Mount Fuji: page 140, Torsakarin/iStock/Getty Images Plus
Table Mountain: page 145, Alexcpt/iStock/Getty Images Plus

INDEX

A

Abeyta, Don Bernardo, 33
Angkor Wat, 138–139
Ásatrúarfélagið, 87, 88

B

Bali, 132–133
Ballyboley Forest, 65
Barrera, Don Julian Santa-
na, 72
Beaumont, Dorothy, 80
Bell, Betsy, 77
Bell, John, 77
Bell Witch Cave, 77
Bhangarh Ruins, 79
Bishop, Bridget, 68
Bonaparte, Joseph, 82
Bonaparte, Napoleon, 34,
82
Bouriette, Louis, 35
Bryant, Page, 136
Buddha, 17
Bulari, Minma, 116

C

Cannock Chase, 74–75
Castles, 7, 15, 19, 52, 80
Cave of the Crystals, 1, 47
Caves, 1, 4, 7, 11, 24, 45,
47, 54, 59, 70, 77, 107,
114–116
Ceques, 127

Chakras. *See also* Earth
chakras
crown chakra, 105, 111,
125
heart chakra, 105, 110,
117
root chakra, 105, 107,
109
sacral chakra, 105, 110,
113
solar plexus chakra, 105,
110, 114
third-eye chakra, 105,
111, 122, 127
throat chakra, 105, 111,
120
Chimayó, 29, 33
Churches, 9, 15, 33–35, 54,
69–70, 89, 122–123
City of Ys, 14–16
Corey, Giles, 69
Corpse roads, 127, 129
Crooked Forest, 57
Crown chakra, 105, 111, 125

D

Das, Maharajah Bhagwant,
79
Davelis Cave, 70
Day of the Dead, 87,
98–100
Demons, 15, 23, 69, 73,
85, 87

Devils, 23, 69, 73, 81–82,
90, 144, 146
Devil's Gate Dam, 73
Devil's Peak, 144
Día de Muertos, 87,
98–100
Door to Hell, 1, 60–61
Doyle, Arthur Conan, 146
Dragon Lines, 127
Dragons, 1, 3, 9, 17, 20–21,
24, 81, 144
Dudley Castle, 80

E

Earth chakras. *See also*
Chakras
Glastonbury Tor, 122–123
Great Pyramid, 120–121
Lake Titicaca, 113
Mount Kailash, 125
Mount Shasta, 107–108,
127, 146
Stonehenge, 1, 117–119,
146
Uluru, 114–116
Elves, 23, 88–89
Energy centers, 105. *See
also* Chakras

F

Fairies, 1, 3, 7, 19, 87, 122,
129
Fairy chimneys, 54

Fairy Glen, 7
Fairy lights, 123
Fairy rings, 7
Fairy roads, 127
Fairy village, 54
Fairytale locales
    City of Ys, 14–16
    Fairy Glen, 7
    Giant's Causeway, 1, 11
    Ha Long Bay, 24–25
    Hinatuan Enchanted
        River, 4–5
    Knuckerhole, 9
    Lake Lagarfljót, 20–21
    Llyn y Fan Fach, 27
    Pennard Castle, 19
    Plain of Jars, 12–13
    Strait of Messina, 8
    Swat River, 17
    Yeun Elez, 23
Famadihana, 87, 95, 100
Forests, 1, 4, 29, 57, 65, 74,
    82, 96, 129, 141, 146

G

Gaiman, Neil, 88
Ganges River, 29, 37, 146
Gargam, Gabriel, 35
Ghosts, 64, 68–85, 97, 141
Giants, 1, 3, 8, 11, 12, 144
Giant's Causeway, 1, 11
Glastonbury Tor, 122–123
Good, Sarah, 68
Gorëme, 54–55
Graz, 90–91
Great Pyramid, 120–121
Grottoes, 24, 34

H

Ha Long Bay, 24–25
Hafnarfjörður, 89
Haleakal, 131
Hang Son Doong, 1, 45
Haunted places
    Ballyboley Forest, 65
    Bell Witch Cave, 77
    Bhangarh Ruins, 79
    Cannock Chase, 74–75
    Davelis Cave, 70
    Devil's Gate Dam, 73
    Dudley Castle, 80
    Island of the Dolls, 72
    Ma-no Umi, 81
    New Orleans, 63,
        84–85, 146
    Pantéon de Belén, 64
    Paris Catacombs, 67
    Pine Barrens, 82–83
    Poveglia, 76
    Salem, 63, 68–69
Healing places
    Chimayó, 29, 33
    Ganges River, 29, 37,
        146
    Killin, 29, 40–41
    Kusatsu Onsen, 29–31
    Lourdes, 29, 34–35, 146
    Naag Mandir, 29, 39
    Stardreaming, 29, 38
Heart chakra, 105, 110, 117
Heilige linien, 127
Héricart de Thury, Lou-
    is-Étienne, 67
Herodotus, 120
Hinatuan Enchanted River,
    4–5

Holy Grail, 117, 122
Holy sites, 127
Hubbard, L. Ron, 73

I

In Search of Magic
    dowsing, 142
    dragons, 21
    earth chakras, 109–111
    fairytales, 21
    haunted houses, 69
    healing energy, 35
    ley lines, 142
    nature magic, 48
    purified water, 35
    quicksand, 48
    rituals, 35
    rivers, 21
    stars, 48
    traditions, 100
Island of the Dolls, 72

J

Jackson, Andrew, 77
Jereb, James, 38
Jersey Devil, 82, 146
Jesus, 121
Johnsen, Árni, 89

K

Kamehameha V, King, 101
Khan, Kublai, 81
Killin, 29, 40–41
Kirk, Robert, 89
Knuckerhole, 9
Kukaniloko, 130
Kusatsu Onsen, 29–31
KwaZulu-Natal, 102–103

L

Lady of the Lake, 27
Lake Lagarfljót, 20–21
Lake Taupo, 143
Lake Titicaca, 113
Lakes, 20–24, 27, 46, 53,
    56, 60, 85, 107, 113, 125,
    127, 132, 143
LaLaurie, Madame, 84–85
Latapie, Catherine, 34
Laveau, Marie, 85
Leeds, Deborah, 82
Ley lines
    Angkor Wat, 138–139
    Bali, 132–133
    Haleakala, 131
    Kukaniloko, 130
    Lake Taupo, 143
    Mount Fuji, 141
    Palenque, 135
    Sedona, 136–137, 146
    Table Mountain, 144–145
    Wistman's Wood, 129
Llyn y Fan Fach, 27
Lourdes, 29, 34–35, 146

M

Madagascar, 87, 95, 100
Ma-no Umi, 81
Mari El Republic, 96–97
Meditation, 110, 111, 125
Mexico City, 87, 98–99
Monmouth, Geoffrey of,
    119
Monoliths, 114, 117–119, 122,
    130, 146
Mont Saint-Michel, 52

Moses, 120
Mount Agung, 132
Mount Fuji, 141
Mount Kailash, 125
Mount Mazama, 107
Mount Meru, 132, 138
Mount of Olives, 120–121
Mount Shasta, 107–108,
    127, 146
Mount Sinai, 120
Mountains, 3, 17, 51, 54, 70,
    107–108, 114, 125, 132,
    141–144
Mystical places, 1, 4, 127

N

Naag Mandir, 29, 39
Naito, Tetsuzan, 81
Nath, Baba Balau, 79
Nature magic
    Cave of the Crystals,
        1, 47
    Crooked Forest, 57
    Door to Hell, 1, 60–61
    Gorëme, 54–55
    Hang Son Doong, 1, 45
    Mont Saint-Michel, 52
    Pink Lakes, 46
    Salar de Uyuni, 53
    Sea of Stars, 48–49
    To Sua Trench, 56
    Tianzi Mountain, 51
    Waitomo, 59
New Orleans, 63, 84–85,
    146
Nightmarchers, 127
Ni'ihau, 101

P

Pakal, K'inich Janaab', 135
Palenque, 135
Pantéon de Belén, 64
Paris Catacombs, 67
Parsons, Jack, 73
Past in present places
    Graz, 90–91
    Hafnarfjörður, 89
    KwaZulu-Natal, 102–103
    Madagascar, 87, 95, 100
    Mari El Republic, 96–97
    Mexico City, 87, 98–99
    Ni'ihau, 101
    Reykjavik, 87, 88
    Saidai-ji Temple, 93
    Taipei, 92
Pennard Castle, 19
Pine Barrens, 82–83
Pink Lakes, 46
Plain of Jars, 12–13
Poveglia, 76
Pyramids, 120–121, 130, 135

R

Randall, John, 143
Ratnavati, Princess, 79
Reykjavik, 87, 88
Rituals, creating, 35
Rivers, 3–5, 17, 21, 29, 37,
    40, 73, 96, 146
Robert the Bruce, 40
Robinson family, 101
Root chakra, 105, 107, 109
Ruins, 7, 19, 79, 135

S

Sacbe, 127

Sacral chakra, 105, 110, 113

Saidai-ji Temple, 93

St. Fillan, 40–41

Salar de Uyuni, 53

Salem, 63, 68–69

Sea dragons, 81, 144

Sea of Stars, 48–49

Sedona, 136–137, 146

Serpent lines, 127–130, 143–144

Serpents, 20, 74, 81

Sevra, Singhia, 79

Sinclair, Elizabeth, 101

Singh, Raja Man, 79

Solar plexus chakra, 105, 110, 114

Somery, John de, 80

Songlines, 127

Soubirous, Bernadette, 34, 35

Sphinx, 120

Spirit Lines, 127

Spirits, 3–4, 15, 65, 72, 82–85, 97–98, 103, 107, 113, 141

Springs, 1, 29–30, 34–35, 107, 122, 132, 146

Stardreaming, 29, 38

Still, James, 82

Stonehenge, 1, 117–119, 146

Stones, 12–13, 114, 117–119, 122, 130, 146

Strait of Messina, 8

Swat River, 17

T

Table Mountain, 144–145

Tada, Takeo, 81

Taipei, 92

Temples, 38–39, 92–93, 113, 121, 132, 135, 138

Third-eye chakra, 105, 111, 122, 127

Throat chakra, 105, 111, 120

Tianzi Mountain, 51

To Sua Trench, 56

Tolkien, J.R.R., 89

Traynor, John, 35

Tree spirits, 4

Turingas, 127

U

Uluru, 114–116

V

Volcanoes, 11, 54, 56, 60, 131–132, 141, 143

W

Waitomo, 59

Water, healing, 1, 29–41, 107, 122, 132, 146

Water spirits, 3–4, 15

Watkins, Alfred, 142

Wei-ming, Lu, 92

Whakataka-Brightwell, Matahi, 143

Wistman's Wood, 129

Y

Yeun Elez, 23